Praise for *Writing for the Ear, Preaching from the Heart*

"In *Writing for the Ear, Preaching from the Heart,* Donna Giver-Johnston demonstrates, in highly practical terms, how to craft and preach sermons that go beyond words written on a page to words inscribed on the hearts of listeners. She spells out a method of writing for the ear that involves crafting sermons in the language of today, aiming for fewer words and greater impact as well as incorporating speaking the sermon into the preparation process. In the delivery of the sermon, the preacher is then able to speak a message she has internalized, not merely memorized, freeing her from the manuscript to communicate a message that is clear, connectional, and compelling.

"Giver-Johnston grounds her strategic suggestions in an analysis of our listeners' contexts: declining interest in the church, secular suspicion of the transcendent, and shortened attention spans. She sets her process in the biblical context of the importance of memory and remembrance and the context of historical and current homiletical theories. The result is a valuable roadmap for an 'oral embodied homiletic that can communicate in the current context, creating a dynamic interaction between preachers and listeners.' *Writing for the Ear, Preaching from the Heart* is a fresh, helpful guide for the preacher who yearns to be able to remember her sermon during its delivery and for it to live in her congregation's memory long after she has ceased to speak."

—Alyce M. McKenzie, Le Van Professor of Preaching and Worship, Perkins School of Theology, and director, the Perkins Center for Preaching Excellence at Southern Methodist University

"Donna Giver-Johnston's *Writing for the Ear, Preaching from the Heart* is packed with the wisdom of experience—a step-by-step approach as inspirational as it is practical. The author encourages preachers to take new risks for a new time and then empowers them with the skills and confidence to do it."

—Anna Carter Florence, Peter Marshall Professor of Preaching, Columbia Theological Seminary and ordained minister in the Presbyterian Church (U.S.A.)

"In this beautifully crafted book, Donna Giver-Johnston has provided a deeply practical guide for preaching that genuinely connects with hearers. She teaches well how to create sermons that leap from the preacher's heart to the listener's ear. But this book is far more than simply a preaching manual. Giver-Johnston reveals her own heart for human need, her own ear for the cries of suffering, her own capacity for lament over fractures in our society, and her own tenacious hope in the healing power of the gospel."

—Thomas G. Long, Bandy Professor Emeritus of Preaching, Candler School of Theology

"All who listen to sermons will welcome this contribution to the oral public performance of scriptural interpretation that is the task of preachers today. By recalling this cultural moment, *Writing for the Ear, Preaching from the Heart* calls preachers to embody their words in a way that reaches the imagination of the listener. This book distills immense scholarship without distracting, itself evidence that the task of writing for the hearer creates content that should never be boring. Giver-Johnston has provided an invigorating book for preachers."

—Joy J. Moore, vice president of academic affairs, academic dean, and professor of biblical preaching, Luther Seminary, and an ordained elder in the United Methodist Church

"The Christian faith is an auditory, acoustical affair. As Paul said, 'Faith comes from hearing.' In this lively, heartfelt book, Donna Giver-Johnston encourages us preachers to recover Christian preaching as a miraculous undertaking in which the gospel arises from the heart of the preacher and goes forth to the ears of our listeners, enchanting and engaging them in ways that take us to the heart of the gospel itself."

—William Willimon, professor of the practice of Christian ministry and director of the Doctor of Ministry program, Duke Divinity School

"*Writing for the Ear, Preaching from the Heart* transcends a simplistic tips-and-tricks manual for preaching without notes. Instead, Donna Giver-Johnston composes a theologically rich, spiritually sensitive, and pastorally wise guide for all preachers. She shows us that preaching can meet our shifting cultural landscape and how, from sermon preparation to delivery, we can break down barriers between pulpit and pew."

—Richard W. Voelz, associate professor of preaching and worship, Union Presbyterian Seminary, and author of *Preaching to Teach: Inspire People to Think and Act* (Abingdon, 2019)

"The day after our city was traumatized by a hate-fueled mass shooting at a local synagogue, I visited one of the 135 congregations under my care. I was captivated and comforted on that horrific day by the word of the Lord through its pastor, Donna Giver-Johnston. She launches this sterling handbook for working preachers by recounting the story of that sermon, eventually detailing step-by-step her unique process for preparing and delivering impactful sermons without manuscript or notes. Listen to her. Walk with her. Her sermons stick. Informed by deep engagement with homiletical scholarship, years in fruitful parish ministry, and genuine love for Jesus, this winsome book is rich with wisdom for preachers willing to risk doing something new to better fulfill their marvelous calling."

—Sheldon Sorge, general minister of Pittsburgh Presbytery, former pastor of three congregations, and associate for theology and worship for the Presbyterian Church (U.S.A.)

"Recently, Donna Giver-Johnston shared an event that caused a 'swirl of words' in Pittsburgh. There was so much noise, she realized her call was to listen for the right word to speak. Such a tension in our society today: the exhausting, noisy words of anger and unleashed grief and the need for gospel words in response. Our ears, as a society, are tired. We ache to hear otherwise. Donna Giver-Johnston offers a way forward here; she has me listening."

—Lisa Nichols Hickman, pastor, teacher, and author of
The Worshiping Life, Writing in the Margins,
and *Praying the Alphabet*

"Grounded in Scripture and tradition, in the study of shifting culture and changing homiletical practices, and most of all in the weekly rhythms of congregational preaching, Donna Giver-Johnston provides a lifeline to preachers in *Writing for the Ear, Preaching from the Heart*. She vividly describes an accessible, dynamic method of sermon preparation and presentation and provides helpful exercises to practice these strategies. Giver-Johnston is convinced that the word of God can be spoken in every sanctuary, every week—and her confidence is contagious. This book reminded me that the sermon is no relic of a bygone era: it can be a lived encounter with Christ and an invitation into community."

—Liddy Barlow, executive minister,
Christian Associates of Southwest Pennsylvania

WRITING FOR THE EAR, PREACHING FROM THE HEART

WRITING
FOR THE EAR,
PREACHING
FROM THE HEART

DONNA GIVER-JOHNSTON

Fortress Press
Minneapolis

WRITING FOR THE EAR, PREACHING FROM THE HEART

All scripture quotations, unless otherwise indicated, are from the New Revised Standard Version Bible © 1989 Division of Christian Education of the National Council of the Churches of Christ in the United States of America. Used by permission.

Scripture quotations marked (NIV) are taken from the Holy Bible, New International Version®, NIV®. Copyright © 1973, 1978, 1984, 2011 by Biblica, Inc.™ Used by permission of Zondervan. All rights reserved worldwide. www.zondervan.com The "NIV" and "New International Version" are trademarks registered in the United States Patent and Trademark Office by Biblica, Inc.™

Scripture quotations marked (KJV) are from the King James Version.

Scripture quoted by permission. Quotations designated (NET) are from the NET Bible® copyright ©1996, 2019 by Biblical Studies Press, L.L.C. http://netbible.com All rights reserved.

Scripture quotations marked (NLT) are taken from the Holy Bible, New Living Translation, copyright ©1996, 2004, 2015 by Tyndale House Foundation. Used by permission of Tyndale House Publishers, Carol Stream, Illinois 60188. All rights reserved.

Scripture quotations marked MSG are taken from THE MESSAGE, copyright © 1993, 2002, 2018 by Eugene H. Peterson. Used by permission of NavPress, represented by Tyndale House Publishers. All rights reserved.

William Willimon, "Personification," in *Preaching the Incarnation*, ed. Peter K. Stevenson and Stephen L. Wright (Louisville, KY: Westminster John Knox, 2010), 21–36. Reprinted by permission.

Donna Giver-Johnston's sermons may be viewed at http://cpcba.squarespace.com/sermons.

Cover Design: Emily Harris / Tory Herman

Print ISBN: 978-1-5064-6323-0
Ebook ISBN: 978-1-5064-6324-7

For Brian, Rebecca, and Christian,
whose love is forever written on my heart

TABLE OF CONTENTS

ACKNOWLEDGMENTS

This book would not be possible without the congregations who called me as pastor and worshipped with me as preacher, affirming both my gifts and my growth with grace, including Brick Presbyterian Church (Brick, NJ), Oak Grove Presbyterian Church (Retreat, NJ), First Presbyterian Church of Findlay (Findlay, OH), and Community Presbyterian Church of Ben Avon (Pittsburgh, PA). Thank you! Your appreciation for my connectional way of preaching inspired me to write this book, in hopes that it might encourage and equip other pastors to try writing for the ear and preaching from the heart.

I am appreciative of Fortress Press's dedication to the Working Preacher Books series guided by the belief that God uses good preaching to change lives. I am grateful for Karoline Lewis, who invited me, a working preacher, to write for the series; for Scott Tunseth, who encouraged me to submit a book proposal; and for Beth Gaede, who brilliantly edited my manuscript with critical expertise and continual encouragement. While Beth and I were editing this book, both of our fathers died within the same week. In the midst of our grief, we share in the hope of the resurrection that we have both heard and preached in sermons throughout our lives. While my father,

ACKNOWLEDGMENTS

Nick Giver, sadly will not get to have the first autographed copy of my book I promised him, his pride and love are written between the lines.

Donna Giver-Johnston
Eastertide, 2021

Everything healthy, everything certain, everything holy, if we can find such things, they all need to be emphasized and articulated. For this it is necessary that there be communication between the hearts and minds of men, communication and not the noise of slogans or the repetition of clichés. Communication is becoming more and more difficult, and . . . speech is in danger of perishing or being perverted in the amplified noise of beasts. . . . There is therefore it seems to me every reason why we should attempt to cry out to one another and comfort one another, in so far as this may be possible, with the truth of Christ.

—Thomas Merton, *Cold War Letters*

Thomas Merton, a Trappist monk in the Abbey of Our Lady of Gethsemani, was one of the most influential Catholic authors of the twentieth century. One of his sixty books, *Cold War Letters*, published in 2007, was originally written in 1961–62 to friends and fellow intellectuals and artists. According to the book jacket, "As the world seemed to tumble toward a nuclear apocalypse, Merton sought to create a community of concern that might raise a moral counterweight to the forces of fear and destruction. *Cold War Letters* are Thomas Merton at his best, writing to us at our collective worst."

INTRODUCTION

Memory is the mother of all wisdom.

—Aeschylus

I remember the first time my first serious boyfriend, Brian, took me home to meet his parents. Linda and Al were lovely people, welcoming me with engaging conversation and many questions. I was able to answer their questions with ease, and I tried to think of this inquiry not as an intense interview but simply as a relaxed conversation. That worked well until Linda asked me a question I had never been asked before: "What is the first thing you can remember? What is your earliest memory?" After a long pause, what came to mind was something that happened when I was only four years old. I was playing with my sisters on a neighbor's porch and thought it would be fun to swing from the rungs on the bottom of the mailbox where the newspaper goes. Falling onto the concrete porch below, I split open my chin. I remember the pain and the tears. And I remember sitting on my mother's lap on the car ride to the hospital to get stitches. But what I remember most is her speaking words of assurance and comfort and love. Her words were the key that transformed my earliest memory from trauma to trust.

What is your earliest memory? What specifics do you remember? Whether good or bad, there are some things we never forget—things like our first friend or our first teacher, the first book we read or the first movie we saw, our first win or our first loss, our first kiss or our first heartbreak, our first job or our first house, our first childbirth (graciously, there are some parts we do forget!), and so on. As a mother, I remember my children's first smiles and first steps, their first cute word and first curse word, their first song and the first cake smeared on their face, their first temper tantrum and first trip to the ER, their first day of school and first parent-teacher conference, their first art project that made me smile and their first essay that brought tears of pride to my eyes, their first strike out and first home run, their first choral concert and first acting performance, their first theological conversation and first prayer, and even the first time they brought home a date whom I could ask, "What is your earliest memory?"

As a preacher, I remember many first times in my career, including the first sermon I preached in the chapel of Westminster College, when I shared my summer experience of volunteering at a homeless shelter in Washington, DC. Afterward, a new graduate student, Brian, invited me to go on a Crop Walk to raise money for hunger. We walked six miles together, talking all the way, and kept walking together until we ended up getting married in the chapel two years later (move over eHarmony).

I remember the first time I saw a woman in the pulpit at New York Avenue Presbyterian Church in Washington, DC. At age twenty-two, I finally understood the call I had received from God at age twelve to serve the church. Seeing a woman in the pulpit allowed me to imagine myself as a preacher. In response, I quit my stable government job and went to seminary.

I remember the first time I received a handwritten note in my mailbox at Princeton Theological Seminary that read, "Women shall not preach." And I remember the first time I was convinced that that was not true—in Professor Nora Tisdale's Women's Ways of Preaching course, when I witnessed and celebrated the extraordinary gifts of female preachers.

I remember the first time I preached a sermon that offended someone. During a session (church board) meeting, Nancy scolded me—with a pointed finger—"You will never mention gays from the pulpit again." I took a deep breath, said a quick prayer for help, and then responded, "I am sorry if my sermon offended you, but I am called by God and this congregation to preach the gospel, and that is what I will do. I look forward to talking with you more about this."

I remember the first time I preached a sermon that blessed someone. After worship, Joan shook my hand and said, "Your words are powerful. I heard God speak a word I really needed to hear today. Thank you."

I remember the first time I looked up from the pulpit and saw someone sleeping. And I remember the first time I looked up from my manuscript and saw someone listening intently, hanging on my every word. I remember the first time during my preaching when I heard someone say, "Amen!" (There is a first time for everything . . . even in a Presbyterian church!)

I remember the first time I preached a sermon in the first person. Wearing a hat, I began with "I am Peter" and, through his eyes, told the story of the transfiguration of Jesus. I remember getting a letter from a teenager who said that it was the first time that the Bible came alive for him.

What do you remember about your preaching? Are there some first experiences you had that shaped your preaching and forever changed the way you preach? All of us preachers have experienced turning points that showed us a better way to preach the word of God to the people of God. For me, the most significant change came when I preached without reading a manuscript.

Although I knew some people who preached without a manuscript, I had resisted it. After all, I worked hard on my manuscript, carefully considering each word and constructing every sentence. I placed a high value on getting the words right and telling the story in a certain way, and I was not going to risk veering off the tracks into what seemed to me to be careless, impromptu ramblings and reckless improvisation. But then I was called to serve First Presbyterian Church of Findlay, Ohio, a large church with a sizable sanctuary and an elevated pulpit, with a substantial distance between the people and me. I soon discovered that the polished manuscript from which I read was no longer a help but a hindrance. It had become an obstacle between the congregation and me. I was not able to connect with the people in the pews when reading from a manuscript.

I will never forget the Sunday I tried something different: I looked up from my manuscript and did not look back down to get the next words. What initially felt like an experience of trauma turned into one of trust. I told a story from memory, not worrying about reciting the carefully constructed sentences but just telling the story with the words that came to me in the moment. I knew the story by heart, and so I told it that way. I felt a connection with the people that I had not felt before. I felt a connection with my words—not written on my manuscript but in my mind and heart—trusting my ability to tell the story. I felt a connection with God's word, feeling an energy as the Spirit was moving through my body and my words. I was forever changed.

I will never forget the response I got from the people that Sunday morning: "It was easy to listen to you preach." "It was as if you met us halfway." "It seemed as if you really believe what you are saying." I will always remember the lesson I learned: it is essential in preaching to make connections—between my words and God's word, between the word and the world, between the preacher and the listeners, between my body and the body of Christ, between hearing and doing, between interpretation and inspiration.

Ever since that day, I have preached without a manuscript and without notes and outside of the pulpit. Since then, I am regularly given positive feedback from listeners:

* One longtime church member said, "When you preach to us, I can't check out. I have to stay with you and pay attention because it's as if you are preaching right to me. It is mesmerizing and stimulating."
* One visitor said, "When you preach, the distance between us is shortened. . . . You are not above us but with us, just a few steps ahead, pointing out how God is at work in our lives."
* One couple decided to join our church, driving an hour each way every Sunday, because, they said, "We don't want someone to read their sermon to us. We like how you preach without notes, from the heart. It is so much more personal and powerful."

Since I began preaching without a manuscript, I am often asked, "How do you do it?"

* A veteran pastor in a continuing education class lamented, "My preaching is stale and dry. I write my sermons months ahead of time, and then I read them in the pulpit. It is a chore without joy."

* A new pastor wrote to me, "I need someone to help me address some of my preaching challenges. My sermons read like an article, and my church members say they don't understand what I am saying. Will you be my preaching coach?"
* A church member who is CEO of a company said, "How do you preach without any notes? My presentations would be so much more effective and powerful if I could do that. Can you teach me how to do what you do?"
* A seminary student told me, "I could never preach without notes, but I wish I could to better connect with my congregation."

Given these comments from a variety of people, I have realized that my method of crafting sermons and my style of preaching together connect with people, helping them hear the biblical message as a relevant and relatable word from God to them. It also keeps me fresh and fed, because I am not just reading words but embodying the narrative flow of the sermon and allowing the Spirit her rightful place in the pulpit, helping me preach a more meaningful sermon. For both the preacher and the congregation, this method of preaching stimulates interest, imagination, and inspiration. Most importantly, it induces remembrance.

Memory plays an important role in communicating the story of our faith. Remembering is a central theme in both testaments of Scripture. Moses instructs the people of God to remember that God brought them out of slavery (Deut 5:15); remember the Sabbath (5:12–14); remember to give thanks for blessings (8:10); remember the covenant—to love God with "all your heart, and with all your soul, and with all your might"—and to keep these words in your heart (6:4–6) and remember to "recite them to your children" (6:7); "take care that you do not forget" (8:11); and "remember the Lord your God" (8:18). Moses has led the Israelites through the wilderness and to the brink of the promised land. Moses knows he is not going with them any farther, and so he leaves them with these important words: "Be careful . . . do not forget the things your eyes have seen or let them fade from your heart as long as you live. Teach them to your children and to their children after them" (Deut 4:9 NIV). Memory is the mother tongue of the biblical witness, the language of faith. Jews and Christians gather weekly to remember the stories and promises of their faith in words read and proclaimed.

In the Gospels, Jesus teaches in ways that his followers will remember. At their last supper together, Jesus "took bread, gave thanks and broke it, and gave it to them, saying, 'This is my body given for you; do this in remembrance of me'" (Luke 22:19 NIV). When Jesus was leaving his disciples to ascend to heaven, he commissioned his followers, teaching them and then saying, "Remember, I am with you always, to the end of the age" (Matt 28:20). There is power in remembering. To remember is not just to recite a word but also to recall a promise, evoke a feeling, inspire faith, nurture hope, and communicate love.

And so, with encouragement, I decided to write this book in order to examine my method and explain it to others, with the hope that it would inspire sermons that go beyond words written on a page to words inscribed on the hearts of listeners longing for a life-giving word to remember.

This book, *Writing for the Ear, Preaching from the Heart*, is, as the name suggests, a guide for helping preachers write sermons for the ear so that they can be remembered and preach sermons from the heart, without a manuscript, so that they are memorable.

Here is how the book is arranged.

In chapter 1 ("Aching Ears"), I provide a brief sketch of our shifting cultural landscape and describe how communication, including preaching, has changed over time. With this heightened cultural awareness, I challenge preachers to change their preaching practices in order to communicate in meaningful and memorable ways that connect with listeners today.

In chapter 2 ("Longing Hearts"), I describe how God communicated in revelation and incarnation, how Jesus communicated in embodiment, and how the church communicates in proclamation. With an enhanced theological consciousness, I recommend an oral, embodied homiletic that can communicate in the current context, creating a dynamic interaction between preachers and listeners.

These two chapters, in describing the current context of aching ears and longing hearts, lead us to chapters 3 and 4, which detail the goal of the book: to cultivate homiletical habits reflective of a heightened cultural awareness and enhanced theological consciousness.

In chapter 3 ("Writing for the Ear"), I provide a method for crafting sermons for the ear that speak in the language of listeners today.

In chapter 4 ("Preaching from the Heart"), I detail the process of getting a sermon into the mind, heart, and body so as to free the preacher from the manuscript in order to communicate a message that is clear, connectional, and compelling.

Informed by an awareness of what listeners most need to hear today and grounded in a theology of incarnation, embodiment, and proclamation, this book provides instruction on how to craft sermons for the ear with the fewest, most impactful words and how to preach sermons without notes in order to communicate a message that captures the ears and hearts of the listeners. In a time when attention spans are shortening and church participation is declining, this book provides a proven method for preachers to connect with listeners and to communicate a memorable word. This is a book that describes *why* this method of preaching is needed in the church to help connect with listeners' aching ears today, *what* theological language has the power and presence to speak to people with longing hearts, *how* to write sermons for the ear, and *how* to preach sermons by heart and from the heart. This book will offer practical insights into the art and craft of preaching as part of the Working Preacher Books series, seeking to provide tools to help "engage a complex world and a changing church from the pulpit." In this complex world and changing church, it is my hope that this book will enable preachers to preach sermons that are engaging and memorable.

Memory not only touches individual lives and testimonies of faith but also contributes to transforming the world. The power of memory is not just in looking back but also in looking forward. I remember the first time that I heard about the tragic and equally inspiring story of Malala Yousafzai, who survived an assassination attempt by a Taliban gunman in 2012 and went on to become an outspoken Pakistani activist for female education. Through her words, the memory of her trauma became a powerful tool for change. As the youngest Nobel Prize laureate, she reminds us, "Let us remember: One child, one teacher, one book, and one pen can change the world."[1] She embodies the truth that words are not just to preserve the past but to change the future.

As preachers, our words of proclamation are to be not enshrined but embodied and enacted. Our words are to be not just read or written but remembered. I share the belief of Fortress Press that God uses good preaching to change lives. It is my hope that this book will inspire change in the sermons you write and the way you preach them so that you might help change the world for good—one word, one sermon, one listener at a time.

1

Aching Ears

Communication and not the noise of slogans or the repetition of clichés . . . is becoming more and more difficult, and . . . speech is in danger of perishing or being perverted in the amplified noise of beasts.

—Thomas Merton, *Cold War Letters*

How Events Change Us

I remember the first time as a pastor when my ears ached, really ached. I remember when my ears were bombarded by words that made me feel such an intense pain and sadness and, at the same time, made me desire to hear and communicate words of healing and hope.

On October 27, 2018, eleven people were shot and killed and seven others injured while they were worshipping in the Tree of Life Synagogue in Pittsburgh, Pennsylvania, not far from the Community Presbyterian Church of Ben Avon, where I serve as pastor. People in Pittsburgh were in shock that this could happen in our city, and they were deeply disturbed and grieved as they heard eyewitness accounts of the malevolent words yelled by the killer: "All Jews must die."

This horrendous hate crime received national attention. Former President Donald Trump announced he was coming to Pittsburgh to pay his respects. Despite the requests of many people, including the mayor and several rabbis, that he postpone his trip until after the period of grieving was over and the dead were buried, he still came. One Presbyterian minister, who lived near the synagogue, was in the crowd as the presidential motorcade drove by, and she expressed her lament, crying out, "You are not welcome here. Let us grieve in peace." She was caught on tape, and her cry was broadcast on a local news station. Soon, the incident went viral and was broadcast on all the national networks.

The next thing I knew, our church Facebook page was being inundated with hateful messages of disapproval about what the minister had said, insisting that we should be ashamed to have her as our pastor and demanding that she be removed. Because she had filled our pulpit a few times and these videos were online, people mistakenly concluded that she was the pastor of our church. One hateful message after another filled up our Facebook page and the church website, calling her "Satan" and us "evil" and swearing that we were all "going to hell." Words, words, words—one hateful word after another overwhelmed us. We had to shut down our Facebook page and church website. I knew that if I had aching ears, then so did others. As the pastor, I knew I had to say something in response, and quickly.

I worked hard to find the right words to speak that would not incite more hate speech. After many words, mostly hurtful ones, had been spewed in the name of Christianity, I had to discern what people most needed to hear and how I could capture their attention with the fewest and most impactful words possible. I knew I had to speak truth to power but with words of challenge, comfort, and grace. I strategically constructed one sentence for the Facebook page and a few sentences for the web page, careful not to add more fuel to the fire for people who might be looking for something to criticize and condemn but also taking advantage of the opportunity to witness to our Christian faith expressed in love for all people. I wrote a pastoral letter to church members and another to the parents of children in our preschool, who were fearful that hate speech would lead to hateful actions that would put their children in harm's way. Finally, I carefully and prayerfully crafted a sermon for our congregation, who needed to hear a word of hope and healing, as well as for visitors, some of whom might be coming to our church that Sunday to cause a disruption or even harm.

Let me be clear that the disruption to our church community paled in comparison to the impact on the Tree of Life Synagogue and Jewish congregations and communities in Pittsburgh and throughout the country. The fear that we lived with for a month was only a glimpse of what Jews have lived with throughout the centuries. We were on the very edge of this tragedy, yet still it significantly impacted our community. One of our church members shared that as she worshipped on the Sunday after the shooting, she immediately noticed that our choir was made up of eleven people, the same number of people who were killed at the Tree of Life Synagogue. Throughout the worship service, she was afraid that someone would come in and kill each choir member. Even people who did not experience the trauma firsthand still struggled with its residual effects, wondering how this could have happened, at a place of worship no less. People came to church that Sunday longing for a word to assuage their fears and offer them healing and hope.

In preparing the sermon, I realized that the world today is not unlike the world from 1961 to 1962, when Thomas Merton wrote a collection of letters to friends, activists, artists, and intellectuals, describing the world as one that is inundated with "the noise of slogans or the repetition of clichés," where "communication is becoming more and more difficult, and . . . speech is in danger of perishing or being perverted in the amplified noise of beasts." I share Merton's belief that it is in such a world as this that "everything healthy, everything certain, everything holy, if we can find such things, they all need to be emphasized and articulated. For this it is necessary that there be communication between the hearts and minds of men." And in the midst of this calamity, I recognized that what is needed now more than ever in the Christian context is a preacher who humbly and courageously attempts "to cry out to one another and comfort one another, in so far as this may be possible, with the truth of Christ."[1] I chose these poignant words of Merton's because of their relevance today. A part of the quote will appear as an epigraph for each chapter to help frame the chapter's focus as well as provide continuity throughout the book.

Today, not unlike the time in which Thomas Merton lived, ours is a troubled world. Our ears ache from hearing news reports filled with a steady drumbeat of disease, destruction, and death. We hear them so much we have become numb to the sensation. We almost do not hear them anymore. But then something catastrophic happens—the September 11 terrorist attack; the high school shooting in Parkland, Florida; the Walmart shooting in El Paso; the Tree of Life Synagogue shooting in Pittsburgh; the police killing of George Floyd on the streets of

Minneapolis—and it becomes a kind of tipping point. In the wake of tragedy, people look for strength and succor, answers and assurances. Some turn back to traditional religion, to which people turned in times of trouble in the past. But more likely, they look elsewhere. It is not the same world. The cultural landscape has shifted, moving society away from the church. Multiple worldviews compete for our attention and allegiance. The words Bob Dylan sang in the 1960s, in a time of cultural revolution, ring true today: "The times, they are a-changin'." Today, we live in a noisy world of competing claims for truth, relevance, and attention.

At this point, you may be wondering what this book might say to you about preaching in this present moment. You may not have had a synagogue shooting in your town (or even a synagogue for that matter), or you may not have had a school shooting in your city, or you may not have had racial justice protests involving your congregation. But wherever you are, people are coming to church having just watched or listened to or read on their phones the latest headlines filled with troubling words. They come into the church needing help to control the chaos, or at least to silence the news and violence and vitriol, even if for an hour, searching for a word of truth and peace, hoping to find a way to make sense of what seems senseless. The people who come to worship and listen still respect the pulpit as a holy place from which a preacher can speak a word of life into a world of death.

Words bombard us every day. Some words are noisy, and some words are cheap. And yet words are all preachers have. As ministers of the word, we are compelled to reflect on our call in the current cultural context, asking ourselves, How do we use our words for good? How do we capture ears in an era of noise?

How do we preach in a way to gain a hearing? How do we preach sermons that connect with listeners? How do we cry out and comfort one another with the truth of Christ? How do we preach words that are memorable? All of these questions reveal the most important question needing to be asked today: Does preaching need to change—and if so, how?

Any communication begins with our audience, but in our cacophonous world, for the preacher to identify who listeners are and what they need to hear can be difficult. In *Preaching at the Crossroads: How the World and Our Preaching Is Changing*, David Lose presents preaching not as a problem to be solved but as a mystery to be embraced. He writes, "The context in which we live, move, and have our being in ministry has changed so significantly that I suspect we don't really know what will work to promote a lively engagement with the Christian faith today." One way to find clues, he says, is by "leaning into and listening carefully to the world in front of us."[2] When we do lean in and listen to the world today, what do we hear?

How Culture Has Changed

As we attend to the world today, we detect that our country's culture has changed considerably, resulting in a significant impact on the church. The cultural shift to a secular society has led to a detached association with religion. Postmodernism has led to a decline in church attendance. Our pluralistic community is characterized by diminished attention. The collective impact of such a dramatic cultural shift on the people who do attend church has made for a disconnected audience. But even when this occurs, still we hear the plea of aching ears, longing for a different word, even a death-defying word.

Secular Society: Detached Association

After I finished conducting a memorial service, the funeral director told me this story about a woman he knew who was under
hospice care. In previous conversations with her, he had learned
that she was a Christian and had put her trust in Jesus and was
not afraid to die. When her estranged family members arrived
for a last visit, he reassured them that she believed in Jesus and
was saved and would be given eternal life in God's kingdom of
heaven. He said it was the strangest thing: "They looked at me
as if I was speaking in a foreign language, like they had no idea
what I was talking about, like they had never before heard of
such things."

There was a time when people knew and agreed on what
was true and trusted that God was in control. But the world has
changed. As people associate themselves with secular concerns,
they become more detached from church. Today, we live in a secular world marked by a reliance on humanity and a suspicion of any
narrative that claims to address current challenges. Secularism is
defined by a lack of confidence in the transcendent realm; divinity
is not assumed, and as Walter Brueggemann observed, "God no
longer functions as the primary character in the narrative of our
lives."[3] People are suspicious, asking, "Is God real?" or "Is religion
relevant?" We live in a world that has undergone a seismic cultural
shift, in which multiple worldviews are part of the cultural air
we all breathe. Multiple truths, multiple news sources, multiple
worldviews, multiple gods, and multiple meaningful options vie
for people's time on Sunday mornings and change their associa-
tions from religious to secular.

The religious landscape of the United States continues to
change at a rapid clip. In telephone surveys conducted in 2018

and 2019, 65 percent of American adults describe themselves as Christians when asked about their religion, down 12 percentage points over the previous decade. Meanwhile, the religiously unaffiliated share of the population, consisting of people who describe their religious identity as atheist, agnostic, or "nothing in particular," now stands at 26 percent, up from 17 percent in 2009.[4]

Many people recognize humanity's separation from God as a crisis but have different ways of addressing the problem. Some say strengthening organized religion is the only solution. Others recognize that people outside the church may consider themselves nonreligious and yet have a religious impulse and yearn for the truth. In *The Protestant Era*, Paul Tillich claims that being religious is "no longer a belief in a supernatural being, but rather a state of ultimate concern, which may express itself in secular as well as religious forms."[5] In our secular society, we have seen a rejection of the transcendent religious realm, even as the quest for doing good in the world continues.

Postmodern Age: Decline in Attendance

I was ordained to the ministry of Word and Sacrament in the New York Avenue Presbyterian Church in Washington, DC, a church with a rich history. The history came alive for me when I sat in the front pew, where, it is said, President Abraham Lincoln used to worship. I remember hearing stories of Pastor Peter Marshall, who also served as the US Senate Chaplain and was a renowned preacher. People remember how church members and visitors would start arriving very early on Sunday mornings to get a place in the church. Others would form lines that wrapped around the building, getting close enough to hear his message via the outside speaker. That was in the 1940s, a very different time in the life of the church.

Some people remember a time when churches were full, but the times have changed. Today, we live in a postmodern world in which a single authoritative Truth has been replaced by multiple "truths" constructed by different groups of people with different beliefs. Postmodernism, notes Lose, ushered in an attitude of "thoroughgoing skepticism toward the reigning philosophical, religious, political, and economic assumptions about the nature of reality."[6] Skeptical of legitimizing one particular standard for all, people are asking, "What is true, if anything?" Recently I asked my home virtual assistant, "Alexa, what is truth?" In less than a minute, she provided several answers, including "fidelity to an original or standard," "property of being in accord with or conforming to reality or fact," and "the opposite of falsity." The next time I asked, she responded, "beliefs, propositions or declarative sentences," and "It is sometimes defined in modern contexts as an idea of truth to self." In essence, Alexa's answer was, "Your guess is as good as mine." Today, people expect instant and easily accessed answers to their questions—pithy not pontificating, personal and certainly not preachy, but with plenty of possibilities.

Postmodernism has resulted in people being skeptical that the church has the corner on the truth. According to a Gallup Poll in 1999, 54 percent identified themselves as "religious only," but just ten years later, in 2009, only 9 percent said they were "religious only," yet 48 percent said they were "both spiritual and religious."[7] About a quarter of US adults (27 percent) now say they think of themselves as spiritual but not religious, up 8 percentage points in five years, according to a Pew Research Center survey (2017). In the postmodern age, the Christian church has changed in dramatic, even alarming ways. In *Christianity After Religion: The End of Church and the Birth of a New Spiritual Awakening*, Diana Butler Bass depicts the state of the church in

America in numbers, reporting "a steady decline of actual religious service attendance from 1975 to 2008, falling from 32 to 24 percent." Bass delivers the news that nearly half of Americans have left their childhood faith in favor of another denomination or religion or by dropping any religious affiliation at all.

Whereas blue laws once limited choices of things to do on Sundays to encourage church attendance, people now have a multitude of options. One of the many options is watching football, which has attracted millions of viewers (14.9 million weekly viewers in the 2018–19 season). Sundays are considered "sacred" for football fans, showcasing multiple football games. Some even go so far as to claim that football has replaced traditional religion in the United States. I can almost guarantee a drop in church attendance on Sundays when the Pittsburgh Steelers have a home game. Another option practiced on Sunday mornings is conversing with friends or reading the paper at a local coffee shop or café. When I called one church member who had been absent for a while, she confessed that Sunday was the only day of the week for her family to sleep in. Whether people are turning to sports, Starbucks, or sleeping in, in this postmodern culture we see a steady decline in religious affiliation and church attendance.

Pluralistic Community: Diminished Attention

I make it a practice to spend time with teenagers in the churches I serve. Whether on summer mission trips, in weekly youth group meetings, or through individual conversations, I enjoy being with them. In these conversations, I always learn something new about their world and how they navigate it. If the moment seems right, I ask them what they think about the church and what makes them want to come or not. One young man told me honestly that he loves worship—it speaks to him—but not so much worshipping with his family. He said his brother fidgets and complains that it is boring and wants to do something more exciting, yet his mother longs for the traditional doxology and King James Bible readings and does not appreciate sermon illustrations of current events. He especially appreciates the sermon, he said, even if throughout it he has to elbow his brother and say, "Pay attention!"

Today we live in a world of pluralism in which multiple realities, stories, and worldviews all compete for attention. The people who do attend church do so differently in this day and age. They come with their cell phones and with a different level of attention and way of listening. Reports have measured the profound impact excessive screen time is having on our brains. Researchers have recorded diminished average attention spans—some claiming the average attention span is even less than that of a goldfish. Other researchers debunk these findings, arguing that there is no such thing as an "average attention span"; rather, it depends on the individual and how much the task at hand commands or inspires their attention. It may not be quantifiable, but in this pluralistic and digital community in which we live, we witness a diminished attention to many things, including the church's ancient narrative.

What does capture our attention? In a word, the internet. In *The Shallows: What the Internet Is Doing to Our Brains*, Nicholas Carr describes the internet's drive toward "efficient, automated collection, transmission, and manipulation of information," led by Google's "deep, even messianic faith in its cause." Google, says its CEO, is more than a mere business; it is a "moral force." The company's much-publicized "mission" is "to organize the world's information and make it universally accessible and useful."[8] With answers that are instant, easily accessible, and succinct, Google captures our attention. Google allows us to do multiple searches on multiple devices simultaneously, with multiple and sometimes varying results. Google thrives in a time of pluralism, marked by the coexistence of two or more principles or sources of authority. While some laud the opportunity Google affords us to multitask, others admit it actually results in diminished attention. Today, the Christian story no longer occupies a privileged place in our culture but is just one of many stories to choose from to find meaning; therefore, it is no longer guaranteed our attention.

Contemporary Culture: Disconnected Audience

Our secular society, postmodern age, and pluralistic community do not exist in separate realms; in fact, they overlap significantly. Together they describe a profound cultural shift that has subtly and not so subtly impacted church congregations, resulting in an audience disconnected from the ancient biblical story and its relevance in the world today.

In a 2019 *New York Times* article, opinion columnist Nicholas Kristof describes the state of Christianity in diminishing numbers. He writes, "Perhaps for the first time since the United States was established, a majority of young adults here do not identify as Christian. Only 49 percent of millennials consider themselves Christian, compared with 84 percent of Americans in their mid-70s or older, according to a report from the Pew Research Center. In summary, the U.S. is steadily becoming less Christian and less religiously observant." The question is, Why? A significant reason for the diminishment of the Christian church, Kristof opines, is that certain Christians have allowed exclusive politics to co-opt it. Sadly, he reports, "For some young people, Christianity is associated less with love than with hate."[9] The Christian church, founded on the truths "For God so loved the world that he gave his only Son" (John 3:16) and "Love your neighbor as yourself" (Mark 12:31), is now regarded by many as the institution of judgment, exclusion, and hate.

Part of the reason people do not know the true essence of Christianity may be that people no longer read the Bible. Along with the decline in church attendance, resulting in fewer people hearing the Bible recited, so too fewer people are reading it at home. Diana Butler Bass reports, "Ninety percent of Americans who came of age in the 1960s consider the Bible to be sacred; while only 67 percent of America's youngest adults revere the Bible as holy."[10] Over the years, the Bible has moved from a prominent place as the only book in a house used to teach children to read, to a treasured devotional book from which people read daily words of inspiration, to a place to record family genealogy, and finally to a mere placeholder on the bookshelf. The Bible may well become an artifact that, like a Gideon Bible in a hotel room nightstand drawer, is put away for safekeeping, rarely seeing the light of day.

As biblical illiteracy increases, people rely on others to read and interpret it for them, turning to a source of information that is not always reliable. For many, reading the Bible has been replaced by reading other books, accessing an inexhaustible library online, and listening to podcasts. Krista Tippett, who hosts the public radio program and podcast *On Being*, believes that religious literacy is not just a matter of taking in knowledge: "It's not just what you know, but what you believe and how you live your life differently, how it helps you navigate these great questions of what it means to be human and what it means to live a worthy life."[11] Those who consider themselves "spiritual but not religious" are still seeking answers, but less and less often from the church.

In this secular, postmodern, pluralist culture in which we live, people who used to find meaning in church worship services are disconnected from sources of truth and from reminders of the story of their faith. Fred Craddock describes the current cultural state as one in which "there is no metanarrative—no narrative beyond the individual stories. . . . You have to live with accidents and coincidences, trying to connect what few dots you can. But do not try to make a lot of sense out of it."[12] To not know the biblical narrative is to not know a story about God's relentless love for God's rebellious people, a story that connects an ephemeral existence with an eternal promise.

As we accurately reflect on the seismic cultural shift and its impact on the church, we are realistic about the challenge but still committed to our mission. Lose sounds a hopeful note: "That's my hope for our venture into the unchartered waters of a world that is simultaneously postmodern, secular, and pluralistic: that we might allow our experience in the culture to challenge us and at times chasten us, as well as renew our confidence both in ourselves as preachers and also—and even more so—in the gospel we have been called to preach."[13] Now it is into the aching ears of people today that we preachers are called to speak words that are meaningful and memorable and make a difference in the living of these days. With steadfast confidence, I pose this critical challenge: How then shall we communicate the gospel that we have been called to preach and that our culture needs and wants to hear?

How Communication Has Changed

One way to discover how to preach to people today is to listen to the world around us. As we do, we become aware of how communication has changed—from the spoken word to the printed word to the digital word—and how that has changed our listeners. Finally, we come to better understand how we need to change our preaching in order to speak to aching ears today.

In the ancient Near East, speaking was the dominant medium of communication. As an oral society, people passed down the Judeo-Christian tradition mainly through stories and ritual recitations of sacred texts. The Hebrews taught their faith to their children with this verse: "Hear, O Israel: The Lord is our God, the Lord alone. You shall love the Lord your God with all your heart, and with all your soul, and with all your might. Keep these words that I am commanding you today in your heart. Recite them to your children and talk about them" (Deut 6:4–7). It was a daily declaration of faith. From the very first word, *Shema*, a Hebrew word that means "hear," it is clear that the teaching and inculcating were done through speaking and hearing.

In addition to reciting the *Shema* as part of daily morning and evening prayers, Jews went to the synagogue to hear readings from the Law and the Prophets. In the Gospel of Luke, we read of Jesus going to the synagogue on the Sabbath and reading from the scroll of the prophet Isaiah. After he was done reading the text aloud, Jesus said, "Today this scripture has been fulfilled in your hearing" (Luke 4:16–21). As a first-century Jew, Jesus continued oral-aural instruction throughout his ministry, teaching his disciples, "Very truly, I tell you, anyone who hears my word and believes him who sent me has eternal life" (John 5:24). He also said, "Let anyone with ears listen" (Matt 11:15). Both the Jewish and Christian testaments reflect the oral culture of the time. Stories were passed down orally, from parents to children, from generation to generation. Eventually, the stories were written down and became sacred text.

Scribes copied the words of the Holy Scriptures onto scrolls, although it was a slow, laborious, and costly process; therefore, the scrolls were kept in the safe place of the synagogue. People came together on the Sabbath to hear the spoken word, and for the rest of the week they had to remember what they had heard.

This slow process of transcribing texts from an oral to a written word continued throughout the centuries until an event that changed the world. In fifteenth-century Germany, Johannes Gutenberg invented the printing press, which allowed books to be printed quickly and affordably; in so doing, he started a printing revolution. At first, the church was reticent to adopt this new invention, but in time it was seen as a valuable tool of evangelism. In the sixteenth century, Martin Luther and other reformers took advantage of the printing press to advance their platform "Sola Scriptura," to put the Bible in the hands of the people, and to effectively expand the "priesthood of all believers." Beginning in the sixteenth century, "a great epistemological shift had taken place in which knowledge of every kind was transferred to, and made manifest through the printed page," according to educator and cultural critic Neil Postman, and it became apparent that "to exist was to exist in print" and "learning became book learning."[14] The Bible was now available for people to own as a devotional guide as well as a textbook for teaching reading. Published in 1611, the King James Bible was named for and commissioned by King James VI for the Church of England to be read in churches. As printed copies became available to the public, the King James Version, more so than other biblical translations, began to shape the English-speaking world in significant ways.

The printing revolution eventually made its way to North America, where the written word became the predominant method of learning and form of public expression. The analytical structure of print was utilized by the colonists to give voice to their cry for freedom, but in a linear, rehearsed manner, as in Thomas Paine's *Common Sense*. As Americans modeled their speaking on the written word—addressed to an invisible audience—the discourse became more formal and impersonal, sounding more like a dissertation than a conversation.

Throughout the eighteenth and nineteenth centuries, public expression continued to be influenced by the printed word. This period of time during which "the American mind submitted itself to the sovereignty of the printing press" Postman brands "the Age of Exposition."[15] Exposition, expounding on a writing or speech primarily to convey information or explain, was the dominant mode of expression until the end of the nineteenth century, when the print-based culture began to change, ushering in a new age of communication.

In the twentieth century, the "Age of Show Business" developed thanks to the invention of the television in 1927, which brought into homes both educational and entertainment programs. With the 1969 arrival of the children's TV program *Sesame Street*, education seemed virtually indistinguishable from entertainment. *Sesame Street* mastered the art of making learning fun and education entertaining.

This phenomenon impacted adult programming as well. As Robert MacNeil, executive editor and coanchor of the *MacNeil/ Lehrer NewsHour*, pointed out, "The idea is to keep everything brief, not to strain the attention of anyone but instead to provide constant stimulation through variety, novelty, action, and movement. You are required . . . to pay attention to no concept, no character, and no problem for more than a few seconds at a time." With the experience of being on television, by 1983 it became clear to him that the assumptions controlling a news show are "that bite-sized is best, that complexity must be avoided, that nuances are dispensable, that qualifications impede the simple message, that visual stimulation is a substitute for thought, and that verbal precision is an anachronism."[16] MacNeil asked the question, "Is Television Shortening Our Attention Span?" and answered it affirmatively then—and even more so now.

The "Age of Show Business" has since been eclipsed by the "Age of the Internet." News is no longer limited to an hour-long television program; rather, most people read online newspaper articles or glance at news headlines that come as alerts on cell phones. Today, we are given bite-sized pieces of information, which in the digital age have been shrunk even smaller, to 280 characters in a tweet. Texts with words or abbreviations have been supplanted, for some people, by Instagram and Snapchat, where pictures are posted with the assumption that they are worth a thousand words that do not need to be spoken, written, or even texted.

As communication has changed from oral to written to digital, so too the culture has shifted, resulting in a change in people's religious association, church attendance, and attention spans. The result has been a disconnect between church and society, between preacher and listener.

How Preaching Has Changed

Preaching has changed to try to bridge the gap between the ancient oral tradition and contemporary communication challenges, seeking to be both faithful to tradition and fitting to the culture. Preaching in the church's early centuries was modeled after Greek and Roman oral rhetoric, with the purpose to persuade listeners. In the next few centuries, persuasion gave way to proposition, with the intent to instruct. In the medieval age, Franciscans and Dominicans developed the "university sermon," which featured a theme divided logically into a three-part explanation. The late sixteenth century gave rise to the Puritan plain-style sermon, which begins with the preacher giving a biblical exposition, then moves to a theological interpretation, and ends with a moral exhortation for the hearers to apply the lesson to their lives.

This structured discourse of deductive logic was practiced in the pulpits of the Western church for five centuries. Sermons became "written speeches delivered in a stately, impersonal tone consisting largely of an impassioned, coldly analytical cataloging of the attributes of the Deity."[17] Even when the preachers of the Great Awakening challenged the rational, rehearsed proclamations of God's word, their emotional sermons were easily transposed onto the printed page and published. In 1870, John Broadus's *On the Preparation and Delivery of Sermons* was published and became the primary homiletical textbook for nearly one hundred years. From this text, homiletics students learned how to write a deductive propositional sermon with one guiding subject, which "should be argued persuasively, illustrated to make the abstract concrete and understandable, and applied so that the truth is given explicit relevance for life."[18] The printed deductive proposition became the sermonic form of choice until the late twentieth century. While preferred and well used by preachers, it may have overstayed its welcome in the pulpit.

In the 1970s, preaching was changed significantly by a movement called the "New Homiletic," which focused less on rhetoric and propositions and more on narrative and plot. Five homileticians are considered the pillars of the New Homiletic. Charles

Rice wrote *Interpretation and Imagination* and later *Preaching the Story*, through which he showed how to translate the ancient story into a contemporary one. Henry Mitchell's *Black Preaching* claimed the importance of speaking to the current culture—not just to the rational being but to the whole person. Outlining the optimal flow of a sermon, he said to "start low, strike fire, and end high"—always end with a celebration of God's glory and goodness. Fred Craddock, in *As One without Authority*, adeptly steered homiletics away from authoritative didactic preaching, which had grown dull for listeners. He refashioned the sermon from an intellectual process into an emotional experience as the sermon, using evocative images, unfolds as a story that listeners were invited to be a part of. Eugene Lowry's *The Homiletical Plot* illustrated the narrative flow of a sermon with "Lowry's Loop": introduce the tension, understand the tension, solve the tension, find serenity when the tension is gone, and avoid the tension. In *Homiletic*, David Buttrick described the sermonic structure and detailed the carefully constructed "moves" the preacher should make in a sermon to ensure the congregation would go along with it. All of these methods focused on sermonic form and centered on preaching as storytelling.

While some homileticians, such as Richard Lischer, challenged the claim that narrative is the most effective preaching method, others refined the method to include personal witness and testimony, as do Tom Long in *The Witness of Preaching* and Anna Carter Florence in *Preaching as Testimony*. Feminists like Mary Donovan Turner and Mary Lin Hudson, in *Saved from Silence*, challenged narrow and fixed interpretations of the Scriptures, instead creating space for women's experiences of the Spirit who heralds the good news of ongoing revelation. Over the years, homiletics has acknowledged the power of preaching and sought to transform the way the preacher speaks words to ears aching to hear, albeit in different ways.

In this turn to inductive preaching, homiletics moved away from the restrictive written word to reclaim the spoken word, which is personal and engaging, spontaneous and invitational. The "sermon moment" allows listeners to participate in the oral proclamation. This shift manifested itself in the sermon becoming less monologue and more dialogue between the text and other voices with different experiences and understandings. Homileticians like John McClure in *Roundtable Pulpit* and *Listening to Listeners* and Lucy Rose in *Sharing the Word: Preaching in the Roundtable Church* focused more on the audience's role as participants in the message. In *Preaching as Local Theology and Folk Art*, Nora Tubbs Tisdale outlined an effective method to understand one's congregation in order to preach a relatable word, and in *Prophetic Preaching*, she provided historical witness, practical strategies, and pastoral inspiration for prophetic proclamation that speaks the truth in love to congregations. Cleophus LaRue described the distinctive power of the preacher who believes in and testifies to God's active involvement in the hearer's life experiences in *The Heart of Black Preaching*. In *Performance in Preaching*, Jana Childers and Clayton Schmit called for preaching that brings the sermon to life. Lisa Thompson argued in *Ingenuity* for a (re)imagination of preaching's vibrancy by naming Black women's interpretive approaches that challenge and by claiming the use of personal and communal language that connects with listeners. Leah Schade's *Preaching in the Purple Zone* described a process for engaging current issues in the pulpit to equip preachers to deliver a relevant word to restless people today. In the shifting culture, marked by a rise in postmodernism and a decline in the church, the New Homiletic, claims O. Wesley Allen, is experiencing a "mid-life crisis of sorts."[19] In an effort to reexamine and reassess, Allen, in *The Renewed Homiletic*, postulates that the New Homiletic will not be abandoned, but instead we will see an adaptation of it. In the current cultural climate, preaching will have to continue to change or risk becoming speech that falls on deaf ears.

How Preaching Has Not Changed

Despite the changes in the style and structure of the sermon, the technique remained the same: a manuscript written for the eye, not the ear. Clyde E. Fant, in his classic *Preaching for Today*, argues that since the nineteenth century, sermons, although preached, were prepared for the eye and not the ear. Although these methods were effective for their age, Fant rightly argues, "they have become increasingly less so as culture has shifted its interest." In 1987, when he published his book, Fant issued a challenge to homiletics: "Like a satellite trapped within the gravitational pull of a planet, preaching has been locked into the Gutenberg galaxy. The sermon must break out of this orbit if it is to be able to communicate within its own medium."[20] Fant challenged homiletics to return the sermon to its original medium by recovering its oral roots of proclamation.

Twenty years before Fant, Canadian sociologist Marshall McLuhan spoke a word that resonated with homiletics: "In a culture like ours, long accustomed to splitting and dividing all things as a means of control, it is sometimes a bit of a shock to be reminded that, in operational and practical fact, the medium is the message."[21] The message for homiletics is clear: Form is just as important as content. The delivery is just as important as the sermon. In fact, the delivery is the sermon, not the text.

Influenced by McLuhan's work, his contemporary Walter Ong became a spokesperson for a forgotten era—an oral culture, when human speech was primary. He sought to recover the ancient resources of orality from the Greco-Roman world of classic rhetoric. In the *Presence of the Word*, Ong states, "Writing is a derivative of speech, not vice versa. A truly oral performance . . . not only arises with no reference to writing but seemingly cannot be performed in any way true to its original if the performer so much as knows how to write." He suggests that oral performances have a power that is lost once the words are put to paper: "An oral-aural culture has no records. It does have memory, but this is not the same as records, for the written record is not a remembrance but an aid to recall. It does not belong to us as memory does. It is an external thing."[22] Ong's challenge to homiletics is clear: preachers need to practice the art of oral proclamation, designing and preaching the sermon in a memorable way, spoken for the ear to hear, not for the eye to read.

This new age marked by diminished attention and disconnected audiences is the one in which we live, with listeners who come to church without the patience or even ability to listen in the same way that their grandparents did. Lengthy sermons written as expositions to be expounded are not well received by today's listeners, who expect to be entertained even as they are educated. As Postman rightly observes, "Most Americans, including preachers, have difficulty accepting the truth, if they think about it at all, that not all forms of discourse can be converted from one medium to another." Further, he argues, "It is naïve to suppose that something that has been expressed in one form can be expressed in another without significantly changing its meaning, texture or value." Sermons are an oral art, which, when put into the form of a written manuscript, lose something. Postman concludes by distinguishing poetry from prose: "We may get a rough idea of the sense of a translated poem but usually everything else is lost, especially that which makes it an object of beauty."[23] Sermons, like poetry, cannot be written in one medium and then delivered in another. Something is lost. Not just the meaning but often the listeners are lost as well.

Then what is a preacher to do who wants to connect with listeners? Fant boldly asserts, "I am convinced that much of the stiffness and impersonality of our preaching, the boredom and lack of interest of our hearers, and the feeling of nonparticipation and disinvolvement of our congregations are due to the manuscripted method of preaching." Instead of encouraging preachers to prepare a manuscript, "the art form of homiletics," Fant advocates for recovering the oral tradition to better communicate in our current culture. By now you are no doubt asking, "Can listeners really tell the difference between sermons composed for the ear and sermons written for the eye?" Fant argues that audiences can successfully label a speech as "oral" or "nonoral" in style; furthermore, "listeners find oral speeches to be more understandable, more interesting, more informative, and superior in style."[24] Not only that but memorable. The individual and collective memory of a congregation is plentiful and powerfully enhanced without the interference of a manuscript.

Did our change in attention spans change the way that we communicate, or did the way we communicate change our attention spans? Like the riddle of the chicken and the egg, it does not really matter which came first. What matters is that much has changed in our world and in the lives of our listeners. And yet our predominant prescribed method of preaching has not changed much.

How Preaching Can Change
for Such a Time as This

Notwithstanding the significant contributions the New Homiletic made to preaching, it was founded on two assumptions—that listeners know the Bible and that they can connect the biblical story with their own stories—neither of which is a given today. In *Making a Scene in the Pulpit*, homiletician Alyce McKenzie contends that "in this time when our screens and attention spans have shrunk, preachers are called, not to give up on conveying the larger story, but to invite people into palm-sized segments of it, from there to connect them to the bigger view." Preachers have to make the connection with their listeners, and this is made easier with a shortened version of a story or scene. McKenzie "considers the shifts in attention span in a digital age to be not merely a problem but an opportunity for homiletics. Cell phones, digital devices, and the divided minds they engender are not simply a source of lamentation for the preacher but an occasion to re-envision what the craft of preaching might look like for a time such as this."[25]

Even though Christianity is a serious and demanding religion, it does not have to be dull. Still, even though preachers today strive to capture the attention of their listeners with shorter scenes, entertainment is not the means or the goal. Postman describes a subtle but important distinction: "Enchantment is the means through which we may gain access to sacredness. Entertainment is the means through which we distance ourselves from it."[26] By enchantment, Postman does not mean the preacher puts a magic spell on the listeners. But by reclaiming the oral medium of preaching, the preacher may find that those who listen do so intently and with great pleasure and delight may be better able to "gain access to sacredness" and connect with God.

Seeking to enchant audiences to connect with God, we must recover the essential genre of preaching. Fant is convinced that "it is more important to allow preaching to be itself—a living encounter of the living Word with the living situation—than either polished phrases or innovative forms." In a culture of distracted listeners, Fant recommends oral preparation, arguing that it "allows us to enter deeply into meaningful, exciting dialogues with our hearers. It sets us free to concentrate on the real meaning of the Word for the real people who sit before us. For the first time, perhaps, we will actually *see* people and talk *with* people, rather than looking *at* our ideas and talking *about* a subject."[27] Others in the field of homiletics have similarly emphasized the need for sermons to be proclaimed orally. According to Fred Craddock, "Much of the awkwardness and discontinuity created by writing and then oralizing a text can be relieved by preparing orally from the outset." Further, he recommends that the preacher "mentally talk through a message."[28] Eugene Lowry's recommendation is direct and succinct: "Prepare sermons out loud."[29] The New Homiletic's narrative medium can become an even more effective message when delivered orally. In *The Renewed Homiletic*, Lowry testifies, "Martin Luther had it right. Faith is an acoustical affair, and I think the preaching office will profit by continuing to pursue a new hearing."[30]

Today, listeners who come to hear us preach come with ears aching from a world that has changed. This cultural shift has challenged the church, particularly preaching. People come with their ears aching from the turbulent noise and troubling words, but they also come to church with ears aching, desiring to hear a different word—a word of good news, a word they can relate to and remember. And so, some of the questions that we preachers have to struggle with include the following:

* How do we communicate eternal hope to secular listeners who value this world?
* How do we communicate truth to postmodern listeners who doubt the existence of one Truth?
* How do we communicate relevance to listeners shaped by pluralism's marketplace of meanings, which is readily available through digital distraction?
* How can we not so much seek to entertain but to enchant people with connection to the sacred?
* How do we preach using words that are memorable and in a way that connects with our listeners today?

One response to these challenging questions is to change the way we write and the way we preach so that we can make a connection between the word of God and the world, using words that our listeners can remember. But how do we find the words?

The world has changed. The church has changed. Listeners have changed. Communication has changed. Preaching has changed before and needs to change again. I boldly reissue Fant's challenge for homiletics today—to break out of the gravitational pull of the Gutenberg galaxy. I encourage preachers to lay down the written manuscript and pick up the practice of oral proclamation. The manuscript sermon suits the eye but not the ear, especially the aching ears that come into our churches today (or not) in search of a word that speaks to them and that they can remember.

Seeking to understand the changing church, authors such as Brian McLaren have written about this timely topic. In *Everything Must Change*, McLaren describes profoundly interesting conversations he has had with people who suspect that "the religious status quo is broken" and are seeking a method of practicing the Christian faith that is authentic and makes a difference in the world for good. With those who consider themselves religious, spiritual, or none of the above, he reports, "Together we've begun to seek a fresh understanding of what Christianity is for, what a church can be and do, and most exciting, we're finding out that a lot of what we need most is already hidden in a trunk in the attic. Which is good news."[31]

This is good news: the church already possesses much of what is needed to change it, even if these treasures are hidden in the attic. We need only to search the attic, throw open the old chests of oral communication, and rummage through the boxes of the New and Renewed Homiletic. There, I am convinced, we have what we need. In recovering our oral roots, we can reimagine what preaching can be today in order to speak to the ears aching to hear a fresh new word spoken in a familiar way that rings true. But what language shall we borrow? I contend that in our collective homiletical memory, we find an oral homiletic that has the power to speak to people today. There we find a different way of writing (for the ear) and a different way of preaching (from the heart, not from a manuscript) that has the potential and power to speak to ears aching to hear the word of God for the people of God today.

Conclusion

Reflecting on the aftermath of the Tree of Life Synagogue shooting, I came to understand that the hateful words posted on our church Facebook page were not only the noise that made my ears ache, but in their condemnation of the pastor's "unchristian speech," they also revealed the fact that people still turn to the church, albeit in smaller numbers, as a place set apart from the world. They still look to the pulpit, longing for a way to connect the word of God with the world they know all too well.

On that Sunday after the synagogue shooting, many people in Pittsburgh still came to church, less out of a sense of duty and more out of a sense of desperation. They came as troubled and traumatized, worried and wounded people from a violent world. They came with pain and sorrow, with anger and anxiety. They came with questions and more questions: Where is God in this? Why do bad things happen to good people? How can we have faith in today's world? How can the church help change the world for good? They came needing to hear a word of grace, power, and love. And so, for All Saints' Sunday, I wrote a short sermon, with carefully chosen words for the ear, and I preached the sermon without notes, from the heart, a message that I could remember in the hopes that my listeners could too. I ended with these words: "May the saints inspire you and me today and help us to see a different way to talk, a different way to care, a different way to see people as human beings, a different way to live and a different way to love, and a different way to change the world for good, for God, and for all of God's people."

My prayer that day was, "Speak Lord, for your people are listening," for truly I knew that they were.

2

Longing Hearts

There is therefore it seems to me every reason why we should attempt to cry out to one another and comfort one another, in so far as this may be possible, with the truth of Christ.

—Thomas Merton, *Cold War Letters*

I remember the first time I truly understood that the incarnation—God becoming flesh—was not just an ancient historical event or an academic theological doctrine. It was the same day I realized that people do come to church with longing hearts—hearts longing to see God. It was Easter Sunday morning, my first Easter as pastor of Oak Grove Presbyterian Church in central New Jersey. I was young and inexperienced but so excited to proclaim the resurrection of Jesus Christ. I was standing by the front door, ready to welcome people as they came to church. As the first family approached, I raised my hands and announced, "Jesus is risen!" The parents smiled and responded, "He is risen indeed!"

But the little girl looked puzzled. And so I bent down, looked her in the eye, and with a big smile said, "Jesus is risen."

She asked, "Where is he? I want to see Jesus."

I said, touching my hand to her chest, "He is right here in your heart."

She persisted, "When do I get to meet him?"

Grasping at theological straws, I said, "Well . . . Jesus is here with us . . . in spirit."

Crossing her arms in front of her, she precociously insisted, "But I want to see him. I want to touch Jesus."

How Longing Hearts Communicate

All of these years later, I still remember the powerful lesson this little girl taught me, one that has informed my pastoral ministry, and in particular my preaching, ever since. In her innocent insistence, she taught me that people come to church longing to meet Jesus. Although I could not show her Jesus literally, I could homiletically. With my words, I could point to Jesus in the hopes that she would get a glimpse.

She is not alone. Many people in today's culture seek to connect to God, and when they cannot connect inside the institutional church, they go in search of meaningful spiritual encounters beyond the ecclesial walls. In *Belief without Borders: Inside the Minds of the Spiritual but Not Religious*, Linda Mercandante reports on her discovery that one of the primary reasons that a growing number of people leave the church—or keep the church at arm's length—is that they perceive it as being irrelevant to the issues they care about.[1]

Some of those issues are played out on the world stage in real time on their cell phones with twenty-four-hour news feeds (gun violence, fires and floods, political events such as a violent insurrection, a presidential inauguration, a second impeachment trial, and so forth). Some issues impact them personally and deeply, resulting in pain and loss. After a week of being exposed to current and concerning events, people long for the moment when they can encounter God's presence—if not in person then at least in the promise that God cares about the things that they care about and that God is at work in the world transforming evil to good. When preachers do not speak to the issues that break the hearts of their people, it communicates that God does not really care. And nothing could be further from the truth.

Although culture and communication have changed, the scriptural promise that nothing "will be able to separate us from the love of God in Christ Jesus our Lord" (Rom 8:39) has not. That is what needs to be communicated to people's longing hearts today in a language and manner they can understand and embrace. Even at a time when "speech is in danger of perishing or being perverted in the amplified noise of beasts," Thomas Merton's call resonates today: "There is therefore it seems to me every reason why we should attempt to cry out to one another and comfort one another, in so far as this may be possible, with the truth of Christ."[2]

This is our calling as preachers of the gospel. But how do we communicate today in our shifting cultural context? How do we communicate truth and hope to postmodern listeners in a secular society? How do we communicate relevance in a pluralistic panoply of possibilities? How do we communicate a theology that connects with people who are "spiritual but not religious"? In essence, how do we speak their language?

Although the religious landscape has changed, a significant number of people are still affiliated with a Christian denomination.

And when determining which church to attend, one of the most critical factors is the quality of sermons. In this shifting cultural context in which communication has changed, we need a homiletical method that connects ancient words to the contemporary world, that connects distracted listeners to God's abiding presence.

In order to establish a theological basis for the recommended method, we will look at how God has communicated throughout the ages and how the church communicates in order to inform how preaching should communicate to people today who listen with aching ears and longing hearts. I contend that just as God's communication with people has changed over the ages, so too preaching needs to adapt to connect with people in this day and age.

How God Communicates

To recover a preaching language that will communicate the gospel in a compelling way for today's environment, we turn to the Bible, where we find the story of our faith written in the language of love. The Bible is not a book but a library of a variety of genres. It tells the story of God and God's people but in different ways throughout history—in prophecies, parables, and promises. In Scripture, we read of God as an active communicator with God's people—in dreams, declarations, direct encounters, and through disciples. Ever since Jesus commissioned his followers, saying, "Go therefore and make disciples of all nations, baptizing them . . . and teaching them to obey everything that I have commanded you" (Matt 28:19–20), the church has been communicating God's message. But in this century, communication has changed. And people are now questioning if the communication of the church is relevant and relational and real. The questioning reveals the seeking. What Augustine said in the second century is as true, and perhaps even more so, today: "Our hearts are restless . . . until they rest in God." A contemporary version is Bruce Springsteen's lyric, "Everybody's got a hungry heart."

We are not the only ones with longing hearts; God longs for us. God cares about humanity and longs to be in relationship with us. God longs for a way to connect with us and communicate with us. It's been that way since the beginning.

In Word (Revelation)

> In the beginning was the Word . . . and the Word was God.
>
> —John 1:1

"Revelation" is a translation of the Greek word *apokalypsis*, which means to unveil something previously covered or unknown. Although used to denote instances of miraculous divine acts or speech, revelation can refer to any means of divine self-disclosure. Throughout the Bible, we witness a God of revelation.

In the beginning, God created humanity in God's image, and when Adam and Eve were hiding in the garden of Eden, God went looking for them. From the beginning, God has wanted to be in relationship with creation and its creatures—all of its creatures, even those rejected and relegated to the margins. When Sarah banished her servant Hagar and her infant son from her house, God found Hagar in the wilderness and provided for her needs. Hagar became the first person in the Bible to name God, saying, "You are *El-Roi*," and asking, "Have I really seen God and remained alive after seeing him?" (Gen 16:13). The name she gave God, *El-Roi*, means "You are the god who sees." The Bible tells the story of a God who sees God's people and a God who wants to be seen by God's people.

The Bible also tells the story of a God who wants to speak to and be heard by God's people. Even at a time when "the word of the Lord was rare in those days, visions were not widespread," the Lord spoke to Samuel. When the young boy Samuel heard his name being called, he ran to Eli and said, "Here I am, for you called me" (1 Sam 3:1, 5). Eli told him that he had not called Samuel and to go back to sleep. Twice more the same thing happened, and then Eli told Samuel to go back to bed, but when he heard the calling, he should answer, "Speak Lord, for your servant is listening" (v. 9). Samuel did as Eli told him, and when he did, Samuel heard and heeded the word of the Lord. Scripture reveals the lengths to which God will go to communicate divine love and desire to be in relationship with God's people, in a variety of ways, using a multiplicity of words.

God spoke a word of creation: "'Let us make humankind in our image, according to our likeness.' . . . So God created humankind in his image, in the image of God he created them; male and female he created them. God blessed them. . . . God saw everything that he had made, and indeed, it was very good" (Gen 1:26–28, 31).

God spoke a word of liberation from captivity. Through a burning bush, God called Moses, saying, "I have observed the misery of my people. . . . I will send you to Pharaoh to bring my people, the Israelites, out of Egypt" (Exod 3:7, 10). Then God instructed Moses to go to Pharaoh and say to him, "Let my people go" (Exod 9:1). With blood smeared on the doorposts of the Hebrews' houses, God spoke a word of protection; by parting the waters of the Red Sea and saving them from the Egyptians, God spoke a word of deliverance.

God spoke a word of commandment through Moses: "You shall love the Lord your God with all your heart, and with all your soul, and with all your might. Keep these words that I am commanding you today in your heart" (Deut 6:5–6). God instructed Moses that this word be inscribed on clay tablets and on the hearts of the faithful.

God spoke a word of covenant through an angel: "I brought you up from Egypt, and brought you into the land that I had promised to your ancestors. . . . I will never break my covenant with you" (Judg 2:1). And when the people were not faithful, God sent prophets to call them back, to remember the covenant God had made with them.

God spoke a word of correction through the prophet Isaiah: "For they are a rebellious people, faithless children, children who will not hear the instruction of the Lord" (Isa 30:9). Even as the people disobeyed the covenant, God continued to call them back through the prophets.

Even so, God spoke a word of comfort: "Do not fear, for I have redeemed you; I have called you by name, you are mine. . . . Because you are precious in my sight, and honored, and I love you" (Isa 43:1, 4).

Throughout, God spoke a word of commitment: "I will make an everlasting covenant with them" (Isa 61:8). In the words of the prophets, God is revealed as a God of justice and mercy, challenge and consolation. God sent prophets to remind the people that the one who rescued them could be trusted to keep the covenant promises made with them.

Ultimately, God spoke a word of remembrance. As a parental figure whose heart's desire is to be in relationship, God remembered the covenant made with God's chosen people. Despite God's communicating through various means, still the people turned away from God and did not remember the covenant. But God did not lose faith with God's people and, with infinite mercy, kept calling them through the words of prophets and priests. Zechariah revealed God's promise:

> Blessed be the Lord God of Israel. . . .
> as he spoke through the mouth of his holy prophets
> from of old,
> that we would be saved from our enemies. . . .
> Thus he has shown the mercy promised to our
> ancestors,
> and has remembered his holy covenant,
> the oath that he swore to our ancestor Abraham,
> to grant us that we, being rescued from the hands
> of our enemies,
> might serve him without fear, in holiness and
> righteousness
> before him all our days. (Luke 1:68, 70–75)

Throughout the biblical story, God remembered the covenant and communicated divine love in different ways, through different spokespersons, so that God's people would also remember. In both Hebrew and Greek, the verb *to remember* has a deeper meaning than just "to recite." The Hebrew word *zakar* (זָכַר) has the sense of "to call to mind" concerning "human obligations," including instructions and commandments. *Zakar* can also describe God's will "to remember people with kindness, granting requests, protecting, delivering"; to remember "his own covenant with them"; or to reveal "his mercy."[3] The Greek word *mimnēskō* (μιμνῄσκω) is defined as "to remind oneself purposefully," to actively "think of, care for, be concerned about," or be motivated by personal interest and involvement. *Mimnesko* can also mean "to be called to remembrance," as by God.[4] "Remembering" the covenant involves calling to mind and also taking action, loving with all the heart, mind, soul, and strength.

God spoke not just eternal words but relational words. God spoke not just into the created world but to human beings and through human voices. God created humanity in God's image, allowing God to find us, rescue us from the lure of sin, and remind us who we are and whose we are. This God, whom Hagar named *El-Roi*, sees God's people and wants to be seen by God's people. This God, whom Samuel heard speak his name, speaks a word in order to be heard. Throughout the Old Testament, God is revealed as always trying to connect, communicate, and keep God's covenant with God's people, thus confirming the desire to be in relationship with us.

In Word Made Flesh (Incarnation)

> In the beginning was the Word . . . and the Word was God. . . . And the Word became flesh.
>
> —John 1:1, 14

"Word" is the translation of the Greek word logos (λόγος), which can also mean "thought, principle, or reason." In Greek philosophy and theology, *logos* represents the divine plan that is implicit in the cosmos, ordering it and giving it form and meaning. John's Gospel begins with the dramatic announcement that the *logos*-word that was in the beginning as God creating the world and all that is in it is the same *logos*-word that became flesh in Jesus.

In the fullness of time, God spoke a word in order to redeem and restore a fallen humanity created in God's image. God spoke a word that did not just tell but showed the depths of divine love. God's word of love was delivered through an angel to an unsuspecting young peasant woman named Mary, whom the angel called "highly favored." The angel promised, "The Holy Spirit will come upon you, and the power of the Most High will overshadow you; therefore the child to be born will be holy; he will be called Son of God" (Luke 1:35). Aware of the scandal of becoming pregnant before her wedding, still Mary consents to being the *Theotokos* (God-bearer) with a few courageous words: "Here am I, the servant of the Lord; let it be with me according to your word" (Luke 1:38). And with Mary's permission, the eternal word became human flesh through her. God's word becoming flesh was given the name "incarnation" by theologians and accepted as foundational to the Christian faith by councils of the early church.

With these three words, "Word became flesh," John reveals the theological promise at the heart of his Gospel. Theologian Emily Holmes contends that, in fact, the incarnation "is the beating heart of the Christian message: God with us in a human body, Word made flesh in history, the good news proclaimed in Christ."[5] These three words, "Word became flesh," unveil the power of "truly God" and "truly human." Jesus Christ, as the word made flesh, acts as the bridge between God's loving heart and humanity's longing heart.

The incarnation is both a mysterious theological concept and a realized event that has been documented and described throughout the centuries, detailing how the transcendent becomes immanent. In the incarnation, God gives humanity what they long for and more. Theologian Jon Berquist captures this longing: "We are like lovers, longing for the glimpse of the beloved. . . . We want to see, and when we see, we want to touch, to hold our loved one close and feel the warmth. We desire to see God." Not only do humans want to see God, but we want to know something of the mind and heart of God. The "scandal" of God's self-disclosure, of God's allowing humanity to see God "with skin on," expresses the lengths to which God will go to communicate steadfast love. What makes the incarnation so scandalous is that, as Berquist attests, "in choosing an embodied, enfleshed existence that is like humanity and that is in humanity's midst, God lived inside skin for that time with us."[6] According to John 1:14, "The Word became flesh and lived among us . . . full of grace and truth." In beholding God's grace and truth—in the flesh—humans come to know the mind and the heart of God in which God's love for humanity is found.

Throughout human history, people have longed to unlock the mystery of divinity by getting a glimpse of God. "People in Jesus' day and even long afterward, looked at Jesus and felt God's presence," observes Berquist. "It was as if God, who had always been there, was suddenly visible, hearable, touchable, graspable. It was as if God had been born in their midst. In the midst of this world with its wonders and its harshness, God lived in Jesus." In Jesus, they saw God face-to-face: "There is a sense in which God is more visible in Jesus than anywhere else. In Jesus' words, God's voice rings out. The reality of God is felt to be near in Jesus' presence. Wherever Jesus is, God is there."[7] In word *and* in flesh, God communicates the divine heart's desire to be in relationship with God's beloved creation: "For God so loved the world that he gave his only Son" (John 3:16).

Poetically and musically, the incarnation is expressed in the beloved hymn "O Little Town of Bethlehem," sung by faithful worshippers throughout the world on Christmas Eve:

41

How silently, how silently the wondrous gift is given!
So God imparts to human hearts the blessings of his
heaven.
No ear may hear his coming, but in this world of sin,
where meek souls will receive him still, the dear Christ
enters in.

This hymn testifies to the radical truth that the dear Christ who entered into the world at a particular time, in a particular place, did so once and for all, imparting heavenly blessings to human hearts.

The incarnation was the means by which God made possible what God intended from the beginning of creation—to see God's people and to be seen by God's people. This truth was manifested in becoming one of us. God's incarnation clearly reveals God's desire to be in relationship with humanity—to be seen and to speak to human beings and to save them from their sin and restore the covenant—"So God imparts to human hearts the blessings of his heaven." In the incarnation, God spoke a revelatory and relational word—through word *and* flesh, communicating God's desire and the lengths to which God will go to be in relationship with creation and all of humanity. God has always wanted to be in relationship with God's people, and over time, God changed the method of communication—using different types of words through different mouthpieces, and even going so far as to make the word become flesh—so that people could remember God's steadfast love that never changes.

In Flesh Made Word (Embodiment)

> In the beginning was the Word . . . and the Word was
> God. . . . And the Word became flesh and lived among
> us, and we have seen his glory, the glory as of a father's
> only son, full of grace and truth.
>
> —John 1:1, 14

In the beginning of the Gospel of John, we encounter God's revelatory and incarnational nature: *The Word became flesh*. In addition, we encounter a revelation about God's relational nature: *The
Word . . . lived among us.* The Greek verb *skenoo* (σκηνόω), which
literally means "to tent" or "to tabernacle," has been translated
in various ways: "The Word became flesh and lived among us"
(NRSV); "made his dwelling among us" (NIV); "took up resi-
dence among us" (NET); "made his home among us" (NLT);
and "moved into the neighborhood" (MSG). All the translations
reveal God's radical plan to be in relationship with humanity.
The word of God became embodied in the person of Jesus, God's
son. In so doing, God changed the way God communicates with
people by becoming flesh and living among them.

When Christians recite the Apostles' Creed—"I believe in
Jesus Christ, God's only Son our Lord; who was conceived by
the Holy Ghost, born of the Virgin Mary, suffered under Pon-
tius Pilate, was crucified, dead, and buried"—we confess our
belief in the incarnation: God became human, word became
flesh in Jesus. In the Creed, although the life of Jesus is indicated only by a comma that separates his birth and his suffering
and death, Scripture gives witness to the truth that not only did
the word become flesh but it lived among us full of grace and
truth. By moving beyond the stories of the birth of Jesus in a few

chapters in the Gospels of Matthew and Luke, we can see how the incarnation is not just a one-time event limited to a babe in Bethlehem.

In Christian tradition, the term *incarnation* functions most broadly as an undeniable exemplar of divine presence. And yet theologians differ in their technical understanding of its scope. Many feminist and womanist theologians have challenged narrow ontological definitions of the incarnation and have expanded the focus beyond Jesus's person to include his message and mission. According to Emily Holmes, what is important is not his "metaphysical incarnation or much less his maleness." Rather, "what makes Jesus paradigmatic for Christians is the way he lives out and embodies his message of good news to the poor, of rejection of systems of oppression, and of love and liberation by God offered to the most despised." As Jesus lived among us, his words and actions reflected God's love. He embodied God's word by showing grace and telling truth. Holmes rightly argues, "The story of Jesus is as much about the flesh becoming word as it is the Word becoming flesh."[8] In Jesus, the word of God became flesh. And as he lived among us, the earthly flesh of Jesus became the embodied eternal word of God.

Jesus, in the flesh, became the Word by which people were forgiven. To the woman caught in adultery, when not one of her accusers were without sin, Jesus said, "Neither do I condemn you" (John 8:11).

Jesus, in the flesh, became the Word by which people were fed: "Taking the five loaves and the two fish, he looked up to heaven, and blessed and broke the loaves, and gave them to the disciples, and the disciples gave them to the crowds. And all ate and were filled" (Matt 14:19–20).

Jesus, in the flesh, became the Word by which people were healed. When a woman who had been suffering from hemorrhages for twelve years came up behind Jesus and touched his cloak, Jesus felt her touch and said, "Daughter, your faith has made you well; go in peace, and be healed of your disease" (Mark 5:34).

Jesus, in the flesh, became the Word by which people were welcomed. Despite the disciples trying to keep them away, Jesus said, "Let the little children come to me, and do not stop them; for it is to such as these that the kingdom of heaven belongs" (Matt 19:14).

Jesus, in the flesh, became the Word by which people were taught the centrality of love. To answer the lawyer's question about which commandment is the greatest, Jesus answered, "'You shall love the Lord your God with all your heart, and with all your soul, and with all your mind.' This is the greatest and first commandment. And a second is like it: 'You shall love your neighbor as yourself'" (Matt 22:37–39).

Jesus, in the flesh, became the Word by which people were resurrected. Even though Lazarus was dead in the tomb for four days, Jesus reassured the crowd, and then he cried with a loud voice, "Lazarus, come out!" And the dead man came out (John 11:43–44).

Jesus, in the flesh, became the Word by which people, especially marginalized people were included and even worthy of imitation. When Jesus was at dinner at the house of Simon, a woman with an alabaster jar came and anointed him. The other guests objected and wanted her dismissed. But Jesus said, "Truly I tell you, wherever the good news is proclaimed in the whole world, what she has done will be told in remembrance of her" (Mark 14:9).

Jesus, in the flesh, became the word of God. Jesus taught people lessons they could relate to and remember. His words were imprinted on the hearts and minds of his listeners. In the flesh, Jesus's words did not just tell; they showed. They showed God's forgiveness, God's abundance, God's healing, God's welcome, God's commandment to love, God's resurrection power, God's inclusive kingdom. Jesus embodied the words he taught. Jesus, as the word made flesh, embodied God's word and, in so doing, demonstrated the ultimate love of God.

Jesus, in the flesh, became the Word by which people saw God. Scripture reveals the incarnation as the distinctive way God is present in the person of Jesus and also gives witness to the ways in which God is present in the world. Holmes argues, "The writings of the Christian Testament contain ample evidence of this incarnate presence; among others through the poor and hungry and naked, the 'least of these.'"[9] Jesus instructed his disciples that his presence was embodied in those places often overlooked:

> Then the righteous will answer him, "Lord, when was it that we saw you hungry and gave you food, or thirsty and gave you something to drink? And when was it that we saw you a stranger and welcomed you, or naked and gave you clothing? And when was it that we saw you sick or in prison and visited you?" And the king will answer them, "Truly I tell you, just as you did it to one of the least of these who are members of my family, you did it to me." (Matt 25:37–40)

In the bodies of the hungry and thirsty, stranger and naked, sick and imprisoned, Jesus was visible for those with eyes to see. A theology of incarnation and a theology of embodiment testify to the truth that God's word became flesh in Jesus and Jesus's flesh became the living word of God.

In Jesus's words, God could be seen perhaps no place more powerfully than on the cross. Hanging between two criminals, Jesus reassuringly replied to the one who asked for mercy, "Truly I tell you, today you will be with me in Paradise" (Luke 23:43). "If we accept the doctrine of the incarnation," contends theologian John Hick, "we believe that the gracious and yet demanding love that we see in Jesus is, literally and identically, the love of God, expressed most fully in Jesus' atoning sacrifice on the cross."[10] With both his dying body and his life-giving words, Jesus declared forgiveness and showed God's love. Through Jesus's flesh becoming words, we come to a fuller appreciation that the incarnation is not just the word made flesh in the birth of Jesus but also his life and ministry, his death and resurrection, in which he fully embodied the word of God that lived among us full of grace and truth.

From a theology of revelation (God's word in Scripture) to a theology of incarnation (God's word made flesh) to a theology of embodiment (Jesus's flesh made Word), we have seen how God has communicated with God's people throughout the ages. Now as we turn to a theology of proclamation (preachers' words and flesh), we witness how God continues to speak through the church that Jesus called to carry on his message of embodied love to God's people.

How the Church Communicates

Throughout the centuries, the church has borne witness to the truth of the incarnation in Jesus Christ. But the fullness of the incarnational witness is aptly summarized by Holmes:

"Anytime we encounter Christ's body in any form, we brush up against the mystery of the incarnation."[11] The mystery reveals itself in all of the ways that God is embodied in the world and communicates with God's people. One place God is embodied in the world and communicates with God's people is in the church—in the form of its practices, people, and preaching.

In Practices

The church, as the body of Christ, hosts experiences of incarnation. In Christian theology, heavenly grace is reflected in earthly sacraments. The elements of water, bread, and cup become visible signs of an invisible reality so that people can experience God's presence in material form. In the church, sacraments are channels of God's ever-present grace and communicate God's eternal love.

The heart of the matter is that Christianity is an incarnational faith. In its ritual practices, the church embodies its theology. In worship, God's grace is revealed in words read in Scripture, proclaimed in sermon, offered in prayers, and sung in hymns. Just as importantly, God's grace is received through physical contact. Through drops of water trickling down the forehead at baptism or remembrance of baptism, we encounter God's love. With a piece of bread and a drop of wine warming the throat, we taste God's grace. Marked with an ashen cross on the forehead, we receive God's mercy. In one hand extended to another across the aisle, we feel God's peace.

Each of these rituals and sacramental practices transforms visible signs into an invisible reality of God's presence. Using these tangible forms, the church connects the divine sacredness to human senses. In worship and ritual, in sacraments and service, the church connects people with God, one another, and God's beloved world.

Jesus, in the flesh, became the bread of life and the cup of salvation, saying, "'This is my body, which is given for you. Do this in remembrance of me.' And he did the same with the cup after supper, saying, 'This cup that is poured out for you is the new covenant in my blood'" (Luke 22:19–20). By initiating the sacraments of baptism and eucharist, in both speaking the words and performing the practices, Jesus embodies the incarnation in ritual and remembrance.

I witnessed the power of the connection between the incarnational "Word made flesh" and the embodied "Flesh made Word" in sacramental practices at a church where I served. There I met Barbara, a charming and loving five-year-old, who greeted me every Sunday with a big hug. For Halloween one year, she told her mom that she wanted to dress up as Pastor Donna, and so, with a costume stole her mom had made and an offering plate she borrowed from the church, Barbara went trick-or-treating. But this became more than a trick, and more of a treat, as I watched Barbara become more interested in the words and rituals of the church. After much conversation between Barbara's mother and me, we decided that Barbara was ready to receive her first communion. I remember the eager look on her face as I spoke the words, "The body of Christ given for you." After the service, I gave Barbara the remaining half of the loaf of communion bread. She thanked me and headed off to the park for a picnic with her mom and younger brother. Later that afternoon, I received a surprising email from Barbara's mother telling me about their picnic. Barbara, of her own accord, went around the park, holding out the bread and saying to each person, "The body of Christ for you." At the young age of five, Barbara understood enough of the incarnation that she knew it was to be embodied. And so she did. Through her tiny hands and big heart, the word became flesh and the flesh became Word.

In People

God is present in the world as the body of Christ in the church, in its practices and people. Each person is a potential host of the divine, a possible site of an encounter with God. All human beings can participate in the incarnation. "Just as incarnation extends far beyond the body of Jesus and even beyond the bodies of Christians, so too does revelation take place in different times and places and in a wide variety of bodies," claims Holmes. Therefore, "instead of a unique event associated with Jesus or his mother, incarnation is a recurring activity." As participants in ongoing incarnation, human bodies become sites of revelation, revealing and reflecting God's word. As Holmes explains, "Because Jesus is the exemplary sacrament of God, making God visible and present through the incarnation in one particular form, all bodies can be seen as sites of sacramental encounter, as extensions of the body of Christ in the world." Bodies can be sacramental signs of divine grace. Although Jesus is the paramount incarnation of God, other people throughout human history have embodied divinity, and through them, the image of God is revealed in fresh and faithful ways. The church is called the body of Christ for good reason. "When Christians imitate Christ and share his message and practices, they participate in redemption and themselves incarnate Christ," affirms Holmes, and when they do, "Christ can then be seen in the face of every person."[12]

As a pastor, it has become abundantly clear to me that the incarnation is not limited to God becoming flesh in the body of Jesus—or even Jesus, in the flesh, becoming God's word. I have witnessed the incarnation as an embodiment of God's presence in the church, the body of Christ, and in the bodies—and hearts and minds and souls—that make up the church. I remember when I got a particular glimpse into this truth. The day Violet was born, I held her in my arms while I said a prayer with her parents. Four weeks later, her parents, dressed in costumes as Mary and Joseph, along with big sister Lotus dressed as an angel, placed baby Violet in the manger for our Christmas Eve family service. She beautifully illustrated the hymn we sang: "Away in a manger, no crib for a bed, the little Lord Jesus lay down his sweet head," even graciously reflecting our words, "no crying he makes." Weeks later, Violet's mother shared with me that Lotus was still introducing her sister not as Violet but as "my baby sister, Jesus."

Despite God's embodiment in human flesh, throughout the centuries the Christian church has elevated the spiritual realm over the physical, denying and even despising the human body. Still, the psalmist testifies to God's intimate involvement in the making of the human body: "For it was you who formed my inward parts; you knit me together in my mother's womb. I praise you, for I am fearfully and wonderfully made" (Ps 139:13–14). The prologue to John's Gospel clearly reveals the fleshiness of the divine word and witnesses to the goodness of the human body. As Johannine scholar Karoline Lewis contends, "God not only goes where God's people go, but is who they are. . . . God now dwells with us by taking our form, our humanity."[13] That is to say, Jesus can be embodied by any human being.

Humans engaged in mission work can become the hands, feet, heart, and voice of God. The call to be an incarnation of Christ in the world means not to be of one substance with God but to participate in God's mission work, to communicate "for God so loved the world." (John 3:16). Not only with words but in flesh, not only with awe but in actions, Christians help make God's kingdom come, on earth as it is in heaven.

In *Amazing Grace: A Vocabulary of Faith*, Kathleen Norris writes that the incarnation is "not an antique doctrine at all, but reality—or ordinary as my everyday struggles with fears great and small, as exalted as the hope that allows me some measure of peace when I soldier on in the daily round. The incarnation is the place, if you will, where hope contends with fear." The incarnation resonates with her own life. Norris describes the intimacy of incarnation: "When a place or time seems touched by God, it is an overshadowing, a sudden eclipsing of my priorities and plans. But even in terrible circumstances and calamities, in matters of life and death, if I sense that I am in the shadow of God, I find light, so much light that my vision improves dramatically. I know that holiness is near."[14] One of these incarnational places—"where hope contends with fear" and where "holiness is near"—is in the pulpit, where the preacher embodies the word of God.

In Preaching

The word that is incarnate in Christ is also encountered in Scripture as it is read, interpreted, and preached. As the written words of Scripture become the spoken words of sermon, preachers participate in the incarnation, making the word flesh. In religious practices such as preaching, there is a form of "divine exchange," Holmes contends, in which "God became flesh so that their flesh might become embodied divine word."[15]

In this way, God still communicates with God's people through the proclamation of the word of God. Charles Bartow presents a practical theology of proclamation based on the understanding that the *logos* (word of God) is not *verbum* (word) but *sermo* (speech), not *ratio* (reason) but *oratio* (discourse). He avows, "It is an event of *actio divina* (God's self-performance). It is in fact God's human speech." Therefore, he claims, to understand "the reading of the scriptural text as *spoken* text and the sermon as *spoken* word . . . takes us straight to the theological heart of the matter." In so doing, our attention is appropriately directed to "God's self-disclosure as performative event," which "deploys language and languages, silence and sound, stillness and gesture, anything—even nothing—to its own ends."[16] While the word is God's infinite self-performance, that was not enough for God. Becoming immanent, God came to earth and continues to speak a word to God's people through preaching. "The incarnation of God in Jesus," argues Berquist, "is a story that lives on in the bodies of those who tell the story even to this day."[17] The word of God continues to be made flesh and communicate love to us and through us in preaching. Preaching is a meeting place, a sacred space, a dynamic encounter between God's word and human words. Bartow provides this powerful illustration of the "divine exchange" of preaching:

> When I step into the pulpit of a church, face the congregation, say, "Let us hear the word of God," and then proceed to read from the Bible and to preach, that *is* a performative action. . . . In the pulpit I am no longer simply a private person. I am a public *persona*. I am still myself, no doubt, whatever that may be. But I am not in service to myself. I am not engaged in self-expression. Instead, I am in service to the words and the Word—the people of God would hear. My weeping, melancholic, all unadorned and shattered self is not what people come to church to see and hear. On their faces you can read it: "We wish to see Jesus" (John 12:21). And, for their sakes, I had better hope to see

him too—however terrifying or comforting the prospect of doing that may be.[18]

Bartow's claim that preaching is "God's human speech," both humbling and empowering, is grounded in Christian Reformed theology. As the Second Helvetic Confession witnesses, "The preaching of the Word of God is the Word of God."[19] It is the word of God for the people of God. And let all God's people say, Thanks be to God!

People come to church to hear the word of God not just in words but in flesh. People come with their longing hearts "wishing to see Jesus." In *Her Preaching Body*, Amy McCullough draws a theological link between the body of the preacher and the sermon, the flesh and the word, rightly identifying the sermon as "a moment of embodying the Word." The voice is not the only instrument of preaching. McCullough claims, "The body is central to preaching . . . not one aspect of the proclamation but the vehicle of her task." And whether or not the assembled gathering recognizes it, God is present in the embodied word of the preacher. McCullough's embodied word theology is reflected in the words of the female preachers she interviewed in her study, including Rev. Harris, who testified, "In preaching, you are an embodied word. . . . The word is not just embodied in me. It is in you. It is in all of us."[20]

Historically, the preacher's use of the body, in voice and gestures, was considered to be a matter only of delivery. More recently, however, rather than dividing the preaching task into writing and delivery, the scope of scholarship has broadened into the category of performance. McCullough argues, "Performance asserted the integral and inseparable role embodiment plays in every sermon, from the initial forays into scripture all the way through the final proclamation." Preaching as performance, therefore, "pushes preachers to think beyond the written formulation of a sermon to the critical moment when it is communicated to a congregation."[21] Preaching is greater than the sum of the words written and spoken; it is the preacher's embodied performance of the word of God for the people of God.

Conclusion

> In the beginning was the Word, and the Word was with God, and the Word was God. . . . And the Word became flesh and lived among us, and we have seen his glory . . . full of grace and truth.
>
> —John 1:1, 14

Today, God continues to speak and live among us, full of grace and truth, through the church—the body of Christ on earth—in its practices, people, and preaching.

In a sermon on John 1:1–14 entitled "Personification," acclaimed preacher William Willimon reveals the power and promise of the ongoing incarnation:

> God doesn't just love us; God comes to us, speaks, reveals, reaches out to us when all the while we thought we were reaching out to God. . . .
>
> I think you know this already. That's why you are here this morning . . . You are here hoping to be met by the Word Made Flesh. . . . Thank God that our God did not wait for us to come to God, but came to us, God With Us, Emmanuel.

In a former congregation I had a man who drove an hour each way to be with us Sunday morning. One Sunday I inquired into the reason for his making such an effort to be at our church. I hoped he would answer, "of course, the brilliant preaching."

He didn't. To my dismay he said, "You know, most of your sermons are over my head. I only understand about one out of four of your sermons."

Really? Then why did he keep coming to our church?

"Because," he answered, "almost every Sunday I meet Christ. Somehow, someway, Christ comes to me, speaks to me, and I go away refreshed and more committed to follow Christ."

Thank God our God was not content to be spiritual. Our God got personal. Thanks be to God.[22]

In becoming flesh, God's love was distinctly articulated, lovingly revealed, and personally embodied in Jesus Christ so that people could meet Christ and see and touch Jesus. In so doing, they could come to know the heart of God, which is always longing to connect with and speak to the hearts of God's people. Therein lies our challenge, and our opportunity, as preachers.

3

Writing for the Ear

Everything healthy, everything certain, everything holy, if we can find such things, they all need to be emphasized. . . .

—Thomas Merton, *Cold War Letters*

My Journey

I remember the day I figured out that, in order for me to communicate to the hearts and minds of my listeners, I had to emphasize (write) and articulate (preach) differently. I was standing in a raised pulpit in the expansive sanctuary of a large church with one thousand members. As the associate pastor, I was new to the church and still trying to get to know people and build relationships. As I preached, I read my manuscript—skillfully constructed paragraphs composed of carefully crafted sentences and cleverly chosen words—looking up every once in a while to make sure they were listening. Some were. Some, it was obvious, were not. In that moment, it became painfully clear to me that I was not connecting with them. In addition to the raised pulpit and the distance between the chancel and the pews, the preacher and the people, I realized that my manuscript was yet another impediment standing between the congregation and me. I decided that I needed to remove one obstacle between us—and I knew the church architecture was not changing. I would have to preach without a manuscript. But how?

I was trained in seminary to write out a manuscript; it was the only way I knew how to preach. My sermons were a lot like essays in which I would judiciously construct the point, carefully choosing each and every word. The truth is that I care about words. I like to craft sentences with care and attention so they communicate well. When I write, I provide a good amount of detail, including descriptive adjectives and adverbs. The result is that the sentences are long but satisfying to the eye of the reader. However, they are not as fulfilling to the ear of the listener.

Wanting to be free from my manuscript and to make eye contact with my listeners, the next time I preached I tried to memorize my sermon, but it did not work well. I realized that not only was it arduous to memorize, but it was also awkward to recite my beautifully crafted, lengthy sentences. Neither could the listeners appreciate them. I soon learned that just memorizing a sermon did not enable me to make the connection I was hoping for. It became apparent that the answer was not about memorizing something written for the eye to read but about writing in such a way that people could hear and remember. It was about writing for the ear.

The next time I practiced my manuscripted sermon from the pulpit, I got out my red pen and began to edit. I shortened sentences to phrases. I changed disconnected words to alliterations. I changed multisyllabic words to short, poignant words. I put an X through a carefully detailed story and wrote in the margins, "Tell the story about my hospital visit with Patty." I found that I did my best editing not sitting at the computer but standing in the pulpit, practicing my sermon, not silently writing down words from my mind but speaking words aloud. What I found was that not only was I able to "learn" the sermon, but I also no longer needed the manuscript. The sentences and the story were something that I could embody and remember. And the listeners could too.

The proof is in the pudding, they say. I was thrilled to hear the people respond enthusiastically. They did not just say, "Good sermon, Pastor." Their comments began to change, from superficial to substantive: "Your words were powerful. They spoke to me," "Thank you for reminding me that no matter how hard the journey gets, God is with me," "I can no longer check out during your sermon; I am with you, waiting to hear what comes next because I know there will be a word for me."

Consequently, I began to change my writing. I stopped writing out the whole manuscript. I learned how to attend to transitions and to tell stories without reading them. I also began to shorten sentences and change words to make them easier to remember. I figured that if I could not remember a sentence, then chances were good that my listeners would not be able to remember it either. And that was the point—to communicate in such a way that listeners would remember what was said or how they felt when they heard it and could take with them a word from God. That was over fifteen years ago, and I have been using this method of writing and preaching ever since.

Thomas Merton reminds us, "Everything healthy, every-thing certain, everything holy, if we can find such things, they all need to be emphasized."[1] Preachers are called to proclaim words that are healthy, certain, and holy. Thankfully, we have those words. Jesus said, "I am the way, and the truth, and the life" (John 14:6). The gospel of Jesus Christ contains the holy way, the honest truth, and the promise of abundant life on earth and eternal life in heaven. But these words need emphasis in order to be communicated from the mouths of preachers to the ears of listeners. As the culture has shifted from religious to postmodern to secular, so too communication has changed from oral to print to digital. And in response, the church is challenged to change in order to speak a connectional and com-pelling message. As the church seeks to stay relevant and con-nect with people today, preachers are in search of a language to speak its message. Times have changed. If preaching is to connect with people in this day and age, it also has to change.

With the provocative metaphor I described earlier, Brian McLaren provides a hopeful picture that allows us to imagine how the church can effectively communicate the Christian mes-sage by looking no further than in its own attic. And so that is what I have done. I essentially opened an antique trunk that revealed valuable treasures not to be preserved but practiced. I discovered the ageless words of Scripture and the ancient prac-tices of Greco-Roman orality, which can be repurposed to fash-ion an oral-embodied homiletic that is faithful to tradition but more fitting to the current culture. Responding to the identified need to change the way we communicate in our church today and reflecting a heightened theological consciousness, I have cultivated homiletical habits through a process I call "writing for the ear, preaching from the heart." It recovers the lost art of oral performance and describes a proven method by which the words of the preacher do not just go in one aching ear and out the other but whereby the sermon is imprinted on the longing hearts of listeners today.

Method or Madness?

You might be thinking, this idea of preaching without a manuscript seems unorthodox, even mad or crazy. Before you dismiss it as a contemporary craze, remember that it has deep historical and rhetorical roots. As established in chapter 1, the ancient resources of orality from Judeo-Christian religious recitations and the Greco-Roman world of classic rhetoric shaped an oral culture in which human speech was primary. Throughout the centuries, the sermon has been transformed from its original oral medium into a written manuscript.

But I am guessing the origin of the manuscripted sermon is not the issue for you. You might be resisting what I am proposing because it seems messy and unpredictable, and you were trained and are committed to staying close to the sermonic text. Or you might reject a method that you fear draws attention to your polished performance when you seek to be but a channel of God's grace. I get it. I hear you.

But let us remember that Jesus did not write or read from a script when he taught and proclaimed God's word. And yet Jesus's oral proclamation was so impactful that it was inscribed on the hearts of his listeners until a later time when they recorded it in print. Jesus taught using words that people could hear and remember.

Jesus used parables: "He told them still another parable: 'The kingdom of heaven is like yeast that a woman took and mixed into about sixty pounds of flour until it worked all through the dough" (Matt 13:33 NIV).

Jesus used stories: "There was a man who had two sons . . ." (Luke 15:11–32).

Jesus used poetry: "Blessed are the poor in spirit. . . . Blessed are the meek. . . . Blessed are the merciful. . . . Blessed are the pure in heart" (Matt 5:3–10).

Jesus used repetition: "You have heard that it was said . . . but I say to you . . ." (Matt 5:21–48).

Jesus used short phrases: "I am the light of the world. I am the good shepherd. I am the resurrection and the life" (John 8:12, 10:11, 11:25).

Jesus used intrigue: "'Surely not I, Lord?' He answered, 'The one who has dipped his hand into the bowl with me will betray me'" (Matt 26:22–23).

Jesus used questions: "Which one of these three, do you think, was a neighbor to the man who fell into the hands of the robbers?" (Luke 10:36).

Jesus used illustrations: "Everyone who drinks of this water will be thirsty again, but those who drink of the water that I will give them will never be thirsty. The water that I will give will become in them a spring of water gushing up to eternal life" (John 4:13–14).

Jesus used models of faith: "Truly I tell you, wherever the good news is proclaimed in the whole world, what she has done will be told in remembrance of her" (Mark 14:9).

In Jesus, the word of God became flesh and the flesh became the Word by which people were forgiven, healed, and shown the kingdom of heaven on earth. Jesus knew that in order for there to be communication between the minds of people and the heart of God, he needed to emphasize the extraordinary in ordinary ways.

I know what you are saying—but we are not Jesus. He was the master. He was perfect. But as the hymn "There Is a Balm in Gilead" gently reminds us, "If you cannot preach like Peter, if you cannot pray like Paul, you can tell the love of Jesus, and say, 'He died for all.'" Even if we are not as rhetorically skilled as Peter or as spiritually gifted as Paul, we still have a role to play, a call to preach the word of God. So how do we preach a sermon in the oral tradition that Jesus exemplified?

The answer is not all or nothing—either improvised speech or a printed manuscript. In communications, there is a continuum of orality and literacy, between the spoken and written word. Although over time our culture has moved from oral to literate, Walter Ong restores a sense of balance to the oral-literate continuum by recovering the primarily oral orientations of the Greco-Roman world of classic rhetoric. His work has theological and homiletical implications. On the orality end, we have impromptu sermons that are spoken without any preparation. On the literate end, we have manuscript sermons from which the text is read. Between these two ends of the spectrum, Eugene Lowry identifies "an ongoing and ever-changing tension between orality and textuality, between the human voice and print, between time and space, between event and instruction, between what we hear and what we see."[2] Preachers today can be found at every place on the continuum, and there is often tension— among preachers and within preachers themselves—about the preferred place on the spectrum.

The literate end of the spectrum is anchored firmly by the printed manuscript that is read. It is the method primarily taught in theological seminaries and used by a majority of preachers today. It is sturdy and trustworthy. Once written, the manuscript offers a sense of security, reassuring pastors that even in the face of unexpected pastoral calls and crises during the week, still they will have something to say on Sunday morning. In *Preaching for Today*, Clyde Fant challenges preachers to break out of the Gutenberg galaxy and to move away from reading a printed manuscript. Easier said than done, right?

Another strategy on the literacy end of the spectrum is to write and then memorize the manuscript. That way, you can feel secure that you have words to say, and you can make eye contact with your congregation. However, a preacher who tries to follow a manuscript mentally in the pulpit without having it with them is often a "curious sight," as Fant describes: "When they are successful in recalling the sermon, they sound polished and look poised—sometimes too polished and too poised." However, when they are unsuccessful, "they may get a vacant look on their faces as they rummage around in their mental attics trying to remember all those beautiful phrases they wrote and rewrote in the study. Meanwhile, their mouths have to go on working. But since they aren't too happy about it, they may look slightly irritated, which in turn may cause the audience to wonder what they have done to offend their pastor." Whether successful or unsuccessful in reciting the memorized manuscript, still, claims Fant, "it gives the preaching a curious, disjointed effect."[3] While some preachers can do this well, the memorized script can become like a manuscript, the only difference being that it is "read" internally.

While Fant prefers an oral sermon to a written one, he does not recommend writing a sermon and then trying to memorize an oral version of it. As previously established, writing in one form does not always transfer well to a different form. Preaching is a good example of this. Eugene Lowry argues, "Focusing on memory retention is to rob the hearers of the immediacy of experiencing the gospel proclaimed."[4] To ensure the listeners experience the immediacy of the gospel requires neither a read nor memorized manuscript but instead a creative engagement with the word, both in the preparation process and in the preaching moment. That is done orally.

When preachers have been advised against preparing a written manuscript, often they have gone to the opposite end of the spectrum: giving an impromptu speech without preparation or practice. Of course, some preachers are gifted orators and can "shoot from the hip" and "wax eloquent." But most of us cannot do this well. In fact, the result can be and often is disastrous. As Fant rightly states, "There is nothing more deadly to preaching than the person who can say nothing for thirty minutes, and knows it."[5] No matter how good we think we are at impromptu speaking, this is no ordinary speech. Given that we are proclaiming the word of God, it is important that we honor and take seriously our responsibility to prepare.

So then, if reading a prepared manuscript is not advisable, nor is preaching spontaneously without notes, then what is a preacher to do?

Extemporaneous Preparation

If a sermon is not to be impromptu, then preaching an oral sermon requires extemporaneous preparation. That is to say, the crafting of the sermon is done by speaking the words while preparing it and with the intention of delivering it extemporaneously, without reading a manuscript. Even within this option, a number of possibilities exist.

Sermon Brief

Fant recommends writing an oral manuscript in the form of a sermon brief, which is prepared by asking the following questions:

1. What is the main concern of this sermon (theme, subject, purpose)?
2. What do I want to say about it (points)?
3. What is the form (order)? How do I begin, proceed through movements, and conclude?

The answers to these questions make up a sermon brief, which organizes and simplifies the sermon. A preacher who becomes familiar with the sermon brief can preach without notes. "You will never recall every sentence, but that doesn't matter," claims Fant. "What little you lose in polished phrases—and it will be very little, if you have prepared orally—you will gain in intimate, direct communication with your congregation."[6] This is a good option for preachers who can construct and follow outlines. The benefits are focus, organization, and logical movement. The challenges are thinking in terms of an outline and struggling to recall certain points and moves as you preach. But there are other options besides a written outline.

Road Map

In *Preaching by Ear*, Dave McClellan presents the metaphor of the message as a journey and the various moves of a message as the points on a map. "With this orientation, the preacher, like a traveler, is able to see the entire journey even as the individual steps are being singled out," explains McClellan, "but instead of words, the map is entirely pictographic." Claiming this method is a visual way to remember what comes next, McClellan argues,

66

"This tool or habit plumbs the vast powers of memory that have atrophied through centuries of textual laziness. The oral ancients saw memory (not memorization) as a powerful tool in speech." McClellan affirms, "With a little practice, we can actually visualize the sequence of the sermon on one page much faster than we could artificially memorize the numbered points and subpoints of an outline."[7] In his book, he provides a sample road map of a sermon he preached. While I personally look forward to trying this method sometime, as someone who is artistically challenged (having difficulty even playing Pictionary), I would be afraid that even I would not be able to understand my drawing, let alone be able to explain it to someone else while preaching.

So then, where does that leave us on the orality-literacy continuum? It leaves us in the middle, between impromptu and written manuscript, with an oral preparation that falls between sermon brief and road map. As opposed to impromptu preaching—which is composed, performed, or uttered on the spur of the moment—I am proposing an extemporaneous method in which the sermon is carefully written, for the ear, but delivered orally without notes or text. It is not madness, I claim, as it has served me and my congregations well over the years. And with some practice, it can be learned.

Writing for the Ear

"Writing for the ear" is not a unique method. Many other preachers have used it and homileticians have written about it. Karyn Wiseman argues that writing for the ear—writing that will be heard more than read—is absolutely necessary in theological education and the practice of ministry, but "it is not always considered purposefully." She believes herself fortunate to have observed her father, a United Methodist pastor, at work each week, not writing a sermon, but crafting a "spoken-word event" that was relational, engaging, and connected with his listeners. While admitting that this process may take a little more time, it is well worth the effort. She exhorts preachers, "You will be more engaging and relevant because you are taking the time and making the effort to write in a way that honors who your listeners are."[8] By purposefully attending to the method of "writing for the ear," the preacher's words will have a more profound impact on listeners. The guide and, ultimately, the judge of the sermon composition is the ear of the preacher and the ears of the people aching for a relatable and memorable word.

Wiseman and other contemporary homileticians have recommended writing for the ear, and while this responds to Fant's challenge to break away from the recited written manuscript, still I can hear him asking, "Why do it anyway? Why not prepare for the oral medium in the first place?" I think some people can naturally prepare orally, but most of us cannot. The one leading the homiletical journey wants to ensure that she does not get lost and that he does not lead listeners off the road and end up in a ditch. Personally, I care too much about the clarity of composition and my choice of words to prepare the sermon completely orally. I think there is a way to do both, however. We can write for the ear and preach from the heart (by heart).

My method is a combination: I write a sermon, but I write for the ear, using techniques such as reading it aloud, speaking words and phrases to see how they sound (not what they look like on paper), and continually revising. And then I do the final revising, not on a computer keyboard, but as I practice in the pulpit. I speak the words on the page into life. I speak them aloud and try to internalize the sermon. I try to memorize important sentences to help direct the sermon, but even so, I rework the sentences as I practice and even as I preach to the congregation. The word becomes embodied in me, not just in the preaching moment, but in the weekly process of writing the sermon.

Weekly Process

This hybrid method of sermon preparation maintains the benefits of both writing words and preaching orally. This is not merely an easy way out of sermon preparation. In fact, it cannot be done quickly. It will likely take just as much time as other sermon preparation practices and perhaps even more. But it is well worth the time and effort, for both the preacher and the congregation. My weekly process of "writing for the ear" requires days to read and reflect, write, and revise.

Read and Reflect

This time consists of listening to the scriptural text, biblical commentaries, and congregational context and prayerfully considering how to connect the word of God with the world of the congregation.

Monday: To start the day, I read the Scripture text I will be preaching the next Sunday, prayerfully and orally. Then I take the rest of the day off. This is the day I read other books, articles, and poems—for information and enjoyment and with appreciation for how words are put together. Sometimes I may also work on other writing projects to hone my craft of composition. But mostly, I try to get out of the books and into the world, including walking, swimming, gardening, attending community events, and visiting with family and friends. Whether I am aware of it or not, throughout the day, as I do other things, my mind is ruminating on the selected biblical text.

Tuesday: The first thing I do is read the Scripture text, both silently and aloud, listening to and looking for clues to reveal a message. This begins the exploration of the biblical text. I explore the words and the characters, looking for connections and conflicts. I examine the details to uncover what might be hidden. I notice the narrative: What does it seem to be saying or doing? What word is it speaking to the people then and now? What questions do I have? Throughout the day (and week), I listen for a word from God for my congregation. Depending on the text and the questions I have about it, whether now or later in the week, I may read some critical commentaries to better understand the historical context, literary characters, and theological concepts. I wait until I have some of my own ideas about the meaning of the biblical text before I see what others have said and test my homiletical hunches. The goal is to answer the question, What is the good news according to this text that my particular congregation needs to hear? Once I have identified a theme to reflect on in the worship service, I begin to craft the liturgy, including prayers, hymns, and responses.

Wednesday: Every Wednesday, church members and visitors and I gather eagerly around a table (or a computer screen) for a Bible study. We pray for the illumination of the Holy Spirit and then read the passages for the upcoming Sunday worship. Because I share leadership of the Bible study with church members, sometimes I do more listening than speaking, trying to "read the room" of those gathered around the table and the text. When leading, I may share some of the insights I have gleaned from commentaries to add to the conversation. Throughout the discussion, I listen to which verses are problematic, noticing the tension in the text and attending to the questions that people are asking and the ones they are afraid to ask, where they struggle with this ancient text to hear a relevant word from God.

Thursday: I recite the text and reflect on the Bible study discussion as I go about my ministry, consciously taking the text with me into committee meetings, into the hospital and homes for pastoral visits, into the community for mission work, into the pool as I swim laps at the YMCA, into prayer and meditation time on my yoga mat, and into conversations with my husband as we walk our dog and eat dinner together. He will often ask me, "So, what is the sermon about this week?" It is a good challenge for me to begin to speak what I think I have heard God saying to me even before my thinking is fully formed. I notice what words or verses speak to me, and I choose a focus, or more accurately, it chooses me. At this point, with the deadline of the bulletin looming, I must commit to the claim of the sermon. I revisit the bulletin, making any changes to the liturgy. And I try to decide on a sermon title, which challenges me to put the focus into just a few imaginative and impactful words.

Write

Friday: By Friday, I am ready and (usually) excited to sit down and begin writing the sermon. After days of reading and reflecting, I craft the sermon, aloud and in writing. I start by writing the focus and function of my sermon as a guide to keep me from going off the rails into meandering through multiple different sermons. I read the text again. I think, write some, and speak what I have written; then I think, write some more, and again speak what I have written. The cycle continues as I try to write words that will speak to the ears of my people. I speak as I write to hear how the words sound out loud. After I "finish" a draft of the sermon, then I put it away. I let it sit and simmer, letting the Spirit work on it—and on me.

Let me say a word about "writing" the sermon. I remember when I was at an annual meeting of the Academy of Homiletics, in the elevator heading to a seminar. I said to my friend, "After this, I need to go back to my room and start writing my sermon for Sunday." A man I did not know turned to me and scolded me, "You don't *write* a sermon." I was embarrassed about being called out and did not know what to say. As I recall, he took issue with the verb, arguing for the preferred action of *crafting* a sermon. Having had a few years to ponder his challenge, I now know what to say. For me, writing is not a secular endeavor but a sacred experience. When I write, I am involved in holy conversations. Whether in my head, on a tablet, or at the keyboard, I am writing, and I am praying that the Spirit is present. With this prayerful process, I trust that the words are blessed whether or not we say they have been written or crafted or whatever other preferred word we might use. So when I say that I *write* sermons for the ear, I embrace the word and the process fully, faithfully, and unapologetically.

Revise

Saturday: Finally, I make edits as I listen to how the words sound as I speak them. When the house is asleep and all is quiet, I get up early and read the sermon aloud. And I revise it. I choose words and phrases that flow more easily and sound better to the ear. I make a word road map of the sermon with headings, noting in the margins the journey of the sermon. I work on it for only an hour or so, and then I put it away for the day. But

I continue to replay the words in my head, as I work, play, and rest, throughout the day.

Sunday: I get up early, and as I do yoga, I breathe and try to clear my mind. On my drive to the church, I sing to warm up my voice and I pray to awaken my spirit. Before worship is to begin, I go into the empty sanctuary, stand in the pulpit, and practice my sermon for at least an hour. I speak the words aloud and make revisions. I try to internalize the words and embody the sermon. Some words will stick, others will not. When I preach the sermon to the congregation, I will remember some of my words and release others, trusting that I will receive added words as a divine gift.

Proven Practices

In chapter 4, I will discuss in more detail the Sunday process, including preparation, practice, and performance. But for now, within each of the stages of the weekly writing process—read and reflect, write, revise, and rest—I detail practices that have proven effective. It is my hope that these practices will become homiletical habits that will equip you to engage the method of "writing for the ear."

Read and Reflect

In seminary training, we learned how to read and reflect on scriptural texts and commentaries, which is part of every sermon preparation process. In preparing to write a sermon for the ear, the following practices will enable you to read and reflect on the text, commentaries, and the congregational context in a more intentional and imaginative way.

Personalize: "I know you"

I remember when someone came up to me after a funeral service and said, "I am here with a friend. I didn't know the person who died, but I feel like I do now. You made it so personal."

Personal stories connect with people. Sharing personal stories about ordinary people has relational power. They help the listeners relate to the preacher, the gospel, and even God, helping them imagine themselves in the story of salvation. And people remember them.

Renowned preacher Barbara Brown Taylor reflects in *The Preaching Life* on her sermon preparation process: "Day after day I look at my life, the lives of my neighbors, the world in which we all live, and I hunt the hidden figure, the presence that still moves just beneath the surface of every created thing." She encourages preachers to use this same process, which includes becoming "a detective of divinity, collecting evidence of God's genius and admiring the tracks left for [you] to follow."[9]

To be a detective of divinity requires asking questions and listening to responses. You can start by making a personal connection with people, in the church and beyond, in homes and hospitals, in the community and coffee shops. Then tell their stories back to them, sharing how they reflected God's grace or truth to you. Avoid using sermon illustrations from books or websites. Instead, use what is before you and all around you. See what God is doing in the hearts and lives of people you know. These stories are easy for you to remember and for people to hear. Just make sure you get their permission to share their stories in a sermon.

Nora Tubbs Tisdale made a significant contribution to homiletics with the publication of her book *Preaching as Local Theology and Folk Art.* In it she argues for the importance of not only exegeting the biblical text but also exegeting the congregation. In a basic communication course, students are taught to "know your audience," and likewise, Tisdale gives preachers a method to get to know their congregations and learn the story of the people to whom they deliver their sermons. Sermons personalized by the preacher say to listeners, "I know you," so that as their ears burn with recognition, the message will be meaningful and memorable.

Exercise: Engage in a congregational exegesis to get to know your listeners and understand their cultural context. Consider asking questions like these:

> What stories do they tell? Where are the silences?
> What struggles do they have? What questions do they bring?
> What books or music do they appreciate? Where do they get their news?
> Who are their heroes? Who is marginalized? Who is not in the pews?
> What events get the most attention and enthusiasm? Where is there controversy or conflict?
> What hymns do they love to sing? What rituals do they celebrate or avoid?
> What is their theology—their view of God, Jesus, Spirit, sin, church, mission, salvation?
> What do they find humorous? What do they find troubling?
> What words do they use? What resonates with them? What is holy for them?

I don't mean to suggest that you need to ask all of these questions, but let them guide you to finding your own questions to ask. Once people know that you are interested enough to ask and willing to listen, they will share their stories. And these stories will help you get to know your people so that you can more easily personalize your sermon.

PARTICIPATE: "WE'RE IN THIS TOGETHER"

I remember someone said to me after worship one Sunday, "Thank you for the sermon. I felt like you were talking right to me, like you were in my house this week hearing my questions. How did you know what I really needed to hear?"

Watching and listening are only part of the learning process. At some point, we have to participate in the process. Preaching is no different. It is not a solo endeavor. When researching a sermon, a preacher participates in the ancient conversation of the biblical text and the ongoing conversation of the commentaries. When a preacher invites the current congregation to participate in the conversation, the people can better relate to the text, one another, the preacher, and the sermons. And people remember them.

Homileticians have been challenging the model of the preacher as one who stands over listeners and delivers a message heard from on high. John McClure, in *The Roundtable Pulpit: Where Leadership and Preaching Meet*, and Lucy Atkinson Rose, in *Sharing the Word: Preaching in the Roundtable Church*, both advocate for preaching to be a participatory process in which the preacher and congregation gather around a table to read the biblical text and listen together for a word from God. People bring to the table their particular situations and stories, and they bring to Scripture their particular questions and perspectives. "If we think of a sermon solely on what the preacher creates and delivers," claim Nora Tisdale and Thomas Troeger in *A Sermon Workbook*, "we will have an entirely too narrow understanding of how preaching operates in the hearts and minds of a congregation."[10] The word "liturgy" is from the Greek word *leitourgia*, which literally means "the work of or for the people," originally meaning a public duty, a service undertaken by a citizen. The sermon, as a part of the liturgy, is a work of the people in which both the one in the pulpit and those in the pew participate.

Getting to know the particular perspectives of the congregation does not just happen in worship. The authors of *Listening to Listeners: Homiletical Case Studies* reveal the importance of "listening to the heart, mind, and will of the congregation" and provide pastors with ways to "listen pastorally to the congregation's perceptions of preaching while encountering people in routine ministerial life—in committee meetings, in the hospital, carrying out mission projects, and even in the parking lot."[11] When people feel like their feedback is respected, their concerns are taken seriously, and their questions are valued, they will come to worship with open ears. When they hear that their perspectives are part of the sermon, they will feel connected to the preacher, the church, and God. And they will remember. In *As One without Authority*, Fred Craddock steered preachers away from monological preaching and toward storied sermons, arguing, "Without question, preaching increases its power when it is dialogical, when speaker and listener share in the proclamation of the word."[12]

As I participate in this dialogue, I listen for the effects of the specific time and place, locally and globally, that the congregation and I are living in. A particular occasion will require a particular sermon. For example, a sermon on a baptism or confirmation Sunday can connect the significance of the everlasting promises of God to the people being baptized or confirmed. When there is a tragedy in the community, like the Tree of Life shooting in Pittsburgh or the brutal police killing of George Floyd, a sermon can offer much-needed pastoral care, speaking words of mercy and justice. Preachers who are not afraid to wrestle with difficult questions in the text and speak to disturbing events in the world will nurture a congregation that is willing to listen to a sermon that takes their concerns seriously.

I have regularly used a practice called the Roundtable Pulpit in my ministry. Each Wednesday, a group of church and community members gather together around a table for Bible study. We read aloud, in multiple translations, the Scripture texts that will be recited and preached on that coming Sunday. I listen closely to the questions that people ask and where they struggle to hear the good news. Sometimes if we wrestle with a text, I will acknowledge that in my sermon. For example, "In Bible study this week, we struggled with understanding what God is saying to us." Knowing that people are listening with particular questions and concerns, sermons written for the ear reassure people that "we're in this together," letting them know that their hopes and fears have been heard.

Exercise: Invite a group of people to read the Scripture passage and reflect on it together. Ask questions such as, "What do you wonder about?" "What do you worry about or question?" and "What do you think God's word is saying to us today?" "If you were preaching the sermon on Sunday, what would you say? What do you need to hear?" Use their answers to inform your reflection and shape your sermon so that it is written for their ears.

Write

Having read and reflected on the biblical text and comments from church members and scholars, no doubt you have focused your homiletical hunches, and you are now ready to write. The following practices have proved effective for me and I trust will assist you in writing a more impactful sermon for the ear.

CLARIFY: "THE FOCUS OF MY SERMON IS . . ."

I remember the first time I delivered a sermon in preaching class at Princeton Theological Seminary. I used multiple texts and tried to make several different points, none too well. I remember Professor Tom Long gently but firmly saying, "There is much to say about each text, Donna, but if you just focus on one text, your preaching will be better." Since then, each time I am tempted to use more than one text or try to make multiple points, I remember Professor Long's sage wisdom.

In preaching, it is important to clarify the focus of the sermon—at the beginning, in the middle, and at the end. Remember the old adage: "Tell them what you are going to say, tell them, and then remind them what you told them." When I instructed preaching students at Vanderbilt Divinity School, the first question I asked the listeners during the sermon feedback session was, "What did you hear?" And then I asked the preacher, "What did you want us to hear?" A teaching opportunity presented itself when the answers were not the same. I would guess that for most preachers, the answers to the questions differ more often than they would like. If we want listeners to remember what we preached, we have to clarify the focus of our sermons.

In *The Witness of Preaching*, Tom Long argues for the importance of a clear and compelling claim that points to one biblical text, just as he taught me in our preaching class. He provides a process that includes writing statements of focus and function. A focus statement is "a concise description of the central, controlling, and unifying theme of the sermon"; a function statement is "a description of what the preacher hopes the sermon will create or cause to happen for the hearers." The focus and function statements, Long claims, should come directly from the biblical exegesis (and, I would add, congregational exegesis); they should be related to each other and should be clear. After that, it is equally important to attend to the form of the sermon, which Long describes as "an organizational plan for deciding what kinds of things will be said and done in a sermon and in what sequence."[13] My experience confirms Long's guidance: when I can identify that one thing to say and how to say it, my sermon easily takes form, making it more enjoyable to write and more impactful for listeners.

Most preachers cannot read a passage from Scripture and then, impromptu, get up and preach a good sermon, one in which they or their listeners do not get lost. "Preaching involves plotting," argues David Buttrick, requiring disciplined work, done in stages, by which the preacher "must break the whole meaning into a scenario of moves for speaking." In our current age, in which attention spans are limited and those who occupy our pews are visual learners, the sermon has to move listeners along so that their attention doesn't get sidetracked, lost, or disconnected. Buttrick claims, "Wise speakers know that they have only a few sentences—perhaps three—in which to focus audience attention and to establish what it is they will be speaking." Homiletical forms exist in a variety of methods. Paul Scott Wilson suggests using "four pages of a sermon": tension in the world, tension in the text, good news in the text, good news in the world. John McClure recommends the "four codes"—Scriptural, theological, cultural, and semantic—to weave together in the sermon. In *Preaching*, Fred Craddock provides examples of forms that generate suspense and impact:

problem, solution; what it is not, what it is; ambiguity, clarity; promise, fulfillment. From the beginning and all throughout the creation of the sermon, Buttrick admits, "Designing moves involves theological smarts and rhetorical skill—trained rhetorical skill."[14] And, I would argue, it involves practice and a willingness to try different forms depending on the scriptural text.

Although busy pastors might be tempted to just jump in and start writing, taking the time to write focus and function statements first and to form a structure is a good investment that will pay dividends in clarity for the preacher and congregation. This step makes it easier for people to hear and to follow the sermon, especially in this day of distractions and decreased attention spans. Sermons written for the ear are focused, making them clear and compelling.

Exercise: Ask yourself, "What do I want my listeners to hear me say?" Practice writing a focus statement in less than ten words. Ask yourself, "What do I want my listeners to know/do/feel?" Practice writing a function statement in less than ten words. Ask yourself, "How can I say it?" Practice using a trusted form to plot your moves. Then write your sermon, making changes to clarify your message. After you preach the sermon, ask your listeners, "What did you hear?" and see how close it was to what you hoped they would hear. Remember: choose one text, identify your claim, and be clear about what, why, and how you are saying it. If you do these things before you begin writing, your sermon will be easier to write, and chances are better that your listeners will remember what you said.

WRITING FOR THE EAR, PREACHING FROM THE HEART

Narrate: "Let me tell you a story"

I remember when I learned how to tell stories. When our children were young, my husband and I read storybooks to them before bed. It was a nightly ritual they looked forward to. But what they loved even more than the books was when we would make up a story. "Once upon a time, there was a ranger named Rick," I started one night and went on to weave a web of adventure. I thought it was fun to do once, but the next night, I was surprised when my young son pleaded, "Mom, tell me another story about Ranger Rick." From that time on, I loved to discover the story as I told it. To my great surprise and delight, my now twenty-year-old son says he still remembers the Ranger Rick stories.

A story, at its most basic level, is an account of certain people in certain places doing certain things. In *The Art of Storytelling for Preaching and Teaching*, Stephen Farris claims that a story is simply "the intersection of plot and character," and yet a well-told story has the power "to delight, to teach, or to persuade."[15] People of all ages have been delighted, taught, and persuaded by stories. The Bible contains the greatest story ever told. The preacher is called to tell the story of God's love, in a sermon, with stories. And if the stories are told well, they will be remembered. Our best teacher is Jesus, who told stories to narrate the way, the truth, and the life of salvation. In *The Original Jesus*, N. T. Wright aptly describes the power of stories: "Stories create worlds. Tell the story differently and you change the world. And that's what Jesus aimed to do."[16] In the twentieth century, homiletics moved away from didactic sermons toward narrative sermons so that listeners would be not passive recipients but active participants in telling the story of the sermon. "We can trust the story—as Jesus so obviously did in his parables—to discover and tease out the ways of God," claims Charles Rice. Why? Because the story is trustworthy. "The story is not afraid of irony, contradiction, ambiguity, or playfulness," asserts Rice. In fact, "a good story always has the possibility of telling more than first meets the ear; and there lies the essential, ironic connection between the earthly, recognizably human story and the Word made flesh."[17] Stories are found all around us in the ordinary events of life. The more ordinary it seems, the better able to reveal the extraordinary presence of God.

However, in this time, church attendance has declined, attention spans are diminished, and people, even those raised in the church, are not as familiar with or connected to the biblical story. And even the people who do come to church and listen to sermons are not adept at connecting their stories to the story of Scripture. Tom Long argues that our cultural shift has "eroded our innate story-shaping skills," and we are now experiencing a "cultural deficit disorder" whereby we are "immersed in episodic experiences of life with neither the skill nor the will to look beyond them."[18] Stories are powerful communication tools, but they still require attention to the plot and association with the characters. I do not mean to suggest that telling stories from the pulpit is ineffective; stories can be impactful, but for today's distracted listeners, the preacher needs to make the connections more explicit. Without eliminating storytelling as an effective communication tool altogether, accommodations can be made. One accommodation is to reduce the scale of the story.

While appreciating the power of story in today's cultural context, Alyce McKenzie makes a convincing case that the more effective mechanism in preaching is using a bite-sized scene in which characters and plot are engaging and easier to follow. In *Making a Scene in the Pulpit: Vivid Preaching for Visual Listeners,*

McKenzie suggests, "Life is a lot more interesting when we take time to notice the scenes all around us. So are sermons." Further, McKenzie claims, "It is in a scene, that you capture the hearts and imagination of listeners."[19] A scene that captures the hearts and imaginations of listeners makes a memorable sermon. By focusing on a particular scene with a particular point of view, the preacher helps the listeners enter into the story—and stay there. The practice of writing sermons for the ear demands smaller segments of stories that the preacher can remember and the congregation will find memorable. Sermons written for the ear allow a preacher to invite people to lean in and listen closely, saying, "Let me tell you a story."

Exercise: Practice telling stories. At the dinner table with your family. At the coffee shop with a friend. Even on a walk with your dog. Learn how to create interest with details and pauses. Listen and learn from other good storytellers. When writing your sermon, instead of writing out a story word for word, just write: "tell the story." Practice telling the story by heart.

TESTIFY: "I BELIEVE"

I remember when a church member asked me to testify. I had read Psalm 23 and Romans 8:31–39 as we stood at the grave of her twenty-one-year-old son. As we walked away from the grave, she asked me, "Is the resurrection really true? Will I see my son again?" I said, "Yes, I believe you will see your son again in heaven." She continued pouring out her sorrow: "Nothing makes sense. Tell me something that is true, something I can hold onto." I told her the truest thing I know: "Nothing can separate us from God's love. In life and in death, we belong to God. God is with you now—especially now—and always."

In extraordinary times, when ministering to those at funerals where pain is palpable, and even in ordinary times, when preaching to those with sighs too deep for words, we are asked not for proof or doctrine but for testimony, tried and true. A preacher who is not afraid to tell the truth of what she has experienced of the green pastures *and* the dark valleys of life is one whose words will be heard and remembered and held close to heart. Doctrinal proofs or authoritative maxims do not always connect with listeners today. In a postmodern world, truth is viewed as relative, and numerous claims to it coexist or even compete. Even a preacher with the authority of ordination and a pulpit who claims to have the corner on the truth is suspect. Anna Carter Florence recommends another method in her book, *Preaching as Testimony.* A sermon as testimony is not autobiographical, but it is a "very particular kind of proclamation" in which "the preacher tells what she has seen and heard in the biblical text and in life, and then confesses what she believes about it." Testimony is not something that can be proven true or false; it can only be rejected or believed. "Testimony is confession based and experience fueled; it is a Word of liberation spoken in the face of fear." The first step toward a testimony sermon is to attend to the biblical text. Tending to the text can take many forms, claims Florence: "We can tend a garden or a soup, a hearth or a baby . . . a flock or a ship, a queen or a business. Tending calls for watchfulness and vigilance; it calls for skill and care."[20] After carefully attending to the text, on behalf of the congregation, the preacher speaks truth as he has experienced it; she courageously stands in the face of fear and testifies, "I am not afraid, because I believe God is with us."

Preachers can occasionally invite people to tell their stories, to share what they believe, by giving their testimony in public worship. When I have done this, it has been not only instructive for me but inspiring to others. Having heard other testimonies, they say, "I think I could do that." For the most part, though, the preacher will be the one called to give a testimony in which people can overhear their own testimonies and, through the beliefs of the preacher voiced in sermons, have their own beliefs secured. Sermons written for the ear can help the preacher to testify and the congregation to respond, "I believe."

Exercise: To begin the practice of testimony, you might begin to pay attention—to tend to the story of the biblical text and the stories of those around you and, last but not least, your own story. Try the writing prompt "I believe . . ." and see where it leads you. Tell your testimony, which allows people to hear, remember, and wonder what their story is and how they will tell it.

Revise

After reading, reflecting, and writing the sermon, here are some tried-and-true practices for revising a sermon for the ear: illustrate and emphasize.

ILLUSTRATE: "PICTURE THIS"

I do not actually remember when I first heard it—whether it was written by an English teacher on a mediocre paper, spoken by a preaching professor while giving feedback on a sagging sermon, or spoken by a church member after a less-than-memorable sermon—but I will never forget the wisdom, "Don't tell me, show me." As the old saying goes, "A picture is worth a thousand words." Therefore, rather than telling listeners about something discovered anew in the ancient biblical text, a preacher needs to show them. Words, when put together imaginatively, can paint a picture that is imprinted on the hearts and minds of listeners for years.

This practice has its roots in the Black church, where preachers demonstrate the power of illustrative words and imaginative delivery. "One distinctive hallmark of African American prophetic preaching is its poetic character," claims Kenyatta Gilbert in *Exodus Preaching*. "It not only speaks concretely to situations of tragedy and despair, but it does so in daringly evocative and creative ways, drawing on the beauty of language and culture." In order to do so, preachers must not only value words, asserts Gilbert, but they must also "relish the beauty of how words speak worlds into existence." This attention to how words sound when put together in a poetic way has power. In fact, argues Gilbert, "the African American prophet has had a particular disposition toward using adorned speech to connect with listeners in ways that flattened prose cannot."[21] Teresa Fry Brown describes this adorned poetic language: "Preaching is communication in the concrete, filled with language and images from day-to-day details—dynamic, sights, sounds, smells, tastes, texture, and life scenes."[22]

Poets have a gift for paying attention, and as they describe details with their words, we can picture what they are trying to show us. Acclaimed Black poets illustrate the power of poetic language to reveal deeper truths. In "The Weary Blues," Langston Hughes writes, "In a deep song voice with a melancholy tone / I heard that Negro sing, that old piano moan." In "Who Said It Was Simple," Audre Lorde writes, "There are so many roots to the tree of anger / that sometimes the branches shatter." In "Caged Bird," Maya Angelou writes, "for the caged bird / sings of freedom."[23]

As we preachers know all too well, people may forget what we say, but they will never forget how we made them feel. One person confessed that they were so offended by a detailed joke a preacher used to start the sermon that they did not hear another word he said. Be careful how you use your words—they have power to connect or disconnect people. In order to help people feel connected to the biblical text, the sermon, and ultimately to God, you need to not just tell them but show them. Although preachers may be tempted to overlook revision, it is an important step in the process of transforming words written for the eye (words that inform) to words written for the ear (words that illustrate and illuminate).

In *The Write Stuff: Crafting Sermons that Capture and Convince*, Sondra Willobee describes a way to help preachers illustrate and help listeners picture a scene. She details this "sensory exploration," using the story of the Israelites crossing the Red Sea (Exod 14) as an example:

1. Go through the text with your nose: Do you smell anything? It may be the dank, fishy smell of shallow water . . .
2. Go through the text with your body: Do you feel anything? The heaviness of shoulders and legs that have walked far with heavy burdens . . .
3. Go through the text with your ears: Do you hear anything? Small children whimpering with fear and fatigue . . .
4. Go through the text with your eyes: Do you see anything? A cloud of dust on the horizon raised by the feet of the Egyptian soldiers . . .
5. Do you taste anything? Bile in your mouth because you are afraid.[24]

In order to "show" listeners what we are saying with poetic words that paint pictures, preachers must nurture our imaginations. This takes practice.

Exercise: Try exploring the biblical text of the week through your senses.

1. Go through the text with your nose: Do you smell anything?
2. Go through the text with your body: Do you feel anything?
3. Go through the text with your ears: Do you hear anything?
4. Go through the text with your eyes: Do you see anything?
5. Go through the text with your mouth: Do you taste anything?

Answering these questions will give you a sensory experience of the biblical word. Now use those vivid descriptions in your sermon so the word proclaimed will be an illustrative one that your listeners not only hear but also see and smell, taste and touch. Such a sensory experience will be illuminating, engaging, and unforgettable. Sermons written for the ear have the power of poetic proclamation to help people "picture this."

EMPHASIZE: "LESS IS MORE"

I remember early in my career in ministry, I used to have my husband listen to my sermons on Saturday to offer feedback in preparation to preach on Sunday. One time, as I finished, I asked, "So how was the ending?" He said, "Which one?" We laughed. I edited. And although, for the sake of our marriage, I think that might have been the last time we had our Saturday practice session, I remember to this day the lesson I learned. As one pastoral colleague said, "Cook it until it's done, but don't overdo it." Or, more simply put, "Less is more."

Especially when you are writing for the ear, it is important to emphasize what you want people to remember. This begins by speaking shorter sentences and using words that are less multisyllabic and more informal. As opposed to an analytical, academic essay written for the eye to read, sermons written for the ear to hear need to be written in a colloquial, familiar style. As Barbara Brown Taylor describes her sermon process, "I compose for the ear, not the eye. That means I use the simplest language and syntax I can." Rather than using complicated words and complex sentences, she admits, "I make it sound conversational on purpose, and I try to introduce new images or ideas slowly enough to let them develop in the ear. In a way, my writing is more like transcribing an oral monologue."[25] The practice of using fewer words in a conversational manner has homiletical value. As a preacher, when you simply "say what you mean," your listeners can better "hear what you say."

Sometimes what you want to say is lost to listeners in long sentences without appropriate emphasis. In *A Sermon Workbook: Exercises in the Art and Craft of Preaching*, Thomas Troeger and Nora Tubbs Tisdale share an example of writing in this style, in which each line contains only one brief phrase and the sentences are shorter than in an analytical, academic essay:

> Write for the ear like this:
> Not the long sentences of written prose.
> But brief sentences.
> Words and clauses.
> Each one getting a line.
>
> This is the way we talk.
> The way we listen.
> How we hear.
> Develop your ear for speech.
> How words are heard.
>
> Now and then, you can get away with a longer sentence such as the one you are reading at this moment.

But.
That's written for the eye.
Not the ear.
It makes for hard listening.

And it makes for getting lost while preaching!
Tangled language
becomes tangled revelation,
an obstacle course
for the congregation,
for the heart hungering for God.[26]

The placement of words on the page enables the desired emphasis. This method equips preachers to communicate in a way that creates a positive flow of energy between the preacher and the congregation. "This is a significant matter, as it influences the reception of the sermon because listeners read the faces of preachers as well as listen to their words," argue Troeger and Tisdale. "Preachers buried in their manuscripts are diminishing the delight of interpersonal communication that is part of the power of preaching."[27] Emphasizing less but impactful words is the key to preaching a powerful sermon that is more likely to be heard and understood, as well as remembered.

Exercise: If you are accustomed to writing a full manuscript for the eye, like most of us were trained, the method of "writing for the ear" will take practice. Begin by reviewing one of your sermon manuscripts and revise it. Make long sentences shorter. Circle complicated words and simplify them. Do not worry about writing complete sentences or using correct grammar. Instead of long sentences or complex arguments, use phrases, lists, questions, and alliterations.

Revise the sermon, so instead of long sentences written for
    the eye,
there is only one
brief phrase per line.

The best way of revising is not to read or compose words inside your head but to speak them out loud. Such oral revision of the sermon allows you to hear how it sounds to your listeners, who come with ears aching to hear a word that is meaningful and memorable. Sermons written for the ear tend to be shorter in length, with impactful words crafted in an informal manner, with proper emphasis, trusting that truly "less is more."

Rest

After a baker has worked the dough, she lets it rest, so it can rise. After a chef has grilled a steak, he lets it rest, so it can absorb the juices. After you have poured a glass of red wine, you let it rest, so the flavors can soften. Likewise, after a preacher has written a sermon, it is best to let it rest, so it can breathe in the Spirit. Avoid writing the sermon on Saturday night, but do read through it before going to bed, not to edit it, but just to let the words dwell in your unconscious while you sleep, allowing the word to be written on your mind and heart.

Sermons written for the ear have a better chance of being heard and remembered. I do not mean to suggest that listeners will remember every word preached, but they will find the message meaningful in the way that it makes them think and feel and respond. Reflecting on his long life, a man was asked, of all the meals his loving wife prepared for him, what were his favorites. He said that although he could not remember each and every meal, he does remember being fed, well cared for, full. And grateful. May it be so with the sermons you write for the ear.

Conclusion

My journey, which began years ago with me standing in the pulpit, grasping my manuscript, struggling to communicate with the hearts and minds of my listeners, has led me to a different way of preaching. I hope that my process of "writing for the ear" will help you cultivate homiletical habits that can connect with your listeners and help them connect with God.

To show you where this process might lead, here is a sermon I wrote for the ear on John 14:1–14, "Home Is Where the Heart Is":

Home.
When I say the word *home*, what comes to mind?
A place you grew up. People you love.
Today, for many people, home is not a vacation house or a family reunion.
Home is an order.
We are required to stay home to keep us safe from COVID-19.
Home brings different feelings to us today.
Home today feels a little less like a Norman Rockwell painting and a little more like a Jackson Pollock painting, colorful and messy and scattered.
These days, home may feel less fun and more frantic, less calm and more crowded.
For others, home feels less leisurely and more lonely.
Home is a place where we can't escape the news of the tragic pandemic.
We look to things to soothe us—for some, avoidance; for others, alcohol;

for many of us, Amazon shopping!
At a time when we need it most, we cannot go to our church home, our sanctuary,
to find our hopes renewed.
We are troubled.

Jesus's disciples were troubled.
They hoped that he would be the one—the one to defeat the evil of the world, to rule with righteousness, and usher in the kingdom of heaven.
But their hopes were dashed.
He was preparing to die.
They were troubled.
On the night before his death, he offered them these words of comfort:
"Do not let your hearts be troubled, trust in God, and trust in me.
There are many rooms in my Father's house.
I am going there to prepare a place for you. . . . I will come back and take you to be with me so that you may be where I am."

Jesus promises a place in the Father's house.
What do you think of the Father's house?
Likely, heaven.
But even that brings to mind different images, I learned in Bible study this week.

* One shared her image of heaven was God's house filled with bunk beds.
* For another, it's a beautiful garden with flowers and birds, animals and rainbows.

* One said she is looking forward to being greeted at the pearly gates by her family.
* Another said where there is no longer pain or sorrow, disease or death, but peace.

Whatever your image of heaven, Jesus says there is plenty of room.

"Father's house" is not just a synonym for heaven.
In John's Gospel, location is a symbol of relationship.
In the "Father's house" there are many dwelling places.
The word dwell means "to abide with."
The phrase "dwelling place" does not mean a geographical place or even a gathering of people, and it is not limited to a heavenly home.
The domestic imagery of "abide" means communion, and invites us into a close relationship with God.
Martin Luther says, "God is what you hang your heart upon."
Your grateful and giving heart, yes.
And even your worried heart and your wounded heart, your longing heart and your lonely heart, your troubled heart and your trusting heart.
Home is where the heart is.
Home is where we hang our heart on God.

But how can we find our way there, to a place we could trust enough to hang our heart?
Jesus said, "I am the way and the truth and the life."
"The way" is not a route somewhere but a close relationship with God.
"The truth" is not something we have to prove.

Jesus provides it for us.
"The life" is not something we make for ourselves.
Jesus is the key to opening the gift of life, abundant life on earth and eternal life in heaven,
life abiding with God always.

Jesus said, "No one comes to the Father except through me."
The good news is, through Jesus, everyone can come to the Father.
Through Jesus, everyone can come home. Jesus brings God's home to us, wherever we are.
And Jesus brings us home to our true selves.
It begins in grace. It ends in grace. It's grace. All the way down.
We testify to this way, this truth, this life,
when we sing a beloved hymn that we know by heart.
Sing along with me . . .
"Through many dangers, toils and snares,
I have already come;
'Tis grace has brought me safe thus far,
and grace will lead me home."

4

Preaching from the Heart

Everything healthy, everything certain, everything holy,
if we can find such things, they all need to be emphasized
and articulated. For this it is necessary that there be communication between the hearts and minds of men.

—Thomas Merton, *Cold War Letters*

I remember the first time I had to memorize something to recite
in front of people. In my seventh-grade social studies course, we
had to memorize Abraham Lincoln's *Gettysburg Address.* I began:
"Four score and seven years ago, our fathers brought forth, upon
this continent, a new nation, conceived in liberty, and dedicated
to the proposition that all men are created equal." Whew! I had
gotten through the hard part, the beginning. I took a deep breath
and continued speaking: "Four score and seven years ago, our
fathers brought forth, upon this continent, a new nation, conceived in liberty, and dedicated to the proposition that all men are
created equal." Concentrating hard, I kept going: "Four score and

seven years ago, our fathers brought forth, upon this continent, a new nation, conceived in liberty, and dedicated to the proposition that all men are created equal." I did not notice the giggles in the classroom or the teacher shifting in his seat because all I was focused on was saying the right words: "Four score and seven years ago, our fathers brought forth, upon this continent, a new nation, conceived in liberty, and dedicated to the proposition that all men are created equal." I took a breath, and then I remembered my place and continued speaking: "Now we are engaged in a great civil war, testing whether that nation, or any nation so conceived and so dedicated, can long endure. . . ."

After I was done, I was surprised and embarrassed to learn during the teacher's evaluation that in my recitation I had gotten stuck. He said that I had sounded like a broken record for a while until I got myself unstuck. After my less-than-stellar performance, if someone had told me then that I would become a preacher and would stand up in front of people delivering sermons much longer than the Gettysburg Address, I would have laughed and dismissed them as foolish.

And yet here I am, preaching sermons in front of congregations almost every Sunday since my ordination in 1996. Throughout the years, I have preached in a variety of ways—from reading full, long manuscripts to preaching from notes to using an outline. Today I preach shorter sermons without notes, which I have found to be the most effective method for me and the method most appreciated by my listeners, who come longing for a word that speaks to their heads and their hearts.

How did I make this transition from my seminary training of manuscript preaching to preaching from the heart? The short answer is, slowly and hesitantly. I did not grow up in a religious tradition in which we memorized Scripture verses. Having never done it, I was skeptical of the significance of learning something by heart. When I was a student at Princeton Theological Seminary, though, we were required to take a public speaking class, and Professor Kenda Creasy Dean assigned us the task of learning two Scripture passages to recite to the class. I was terrified, remembering my "broken record" oration of the Gettysburg Address. What was the importance of memorizing anyway, I wondered? We could just read the text from the Bible.

For the class assignment, I chose Psalm 42: "As a deer longs for flowing streams, so my soul longs for you, O God. My soul thirsts for God, for the living God. When shall I come and behold the face of God? My tears have been my food day and night, while people say to me continually, 'Where is your God?' These things I remember, as I pour out my soul" (Ps 42:1–4). I was surprised at how easy it was to remember the psalm. And I was even more surprised that I enjoyed it and found it meaningful, even spiritual. Once I knew the psalm by heart, I could deliver it in a different way—no longer simply reciting words but reaching my listeners with meaning. But the biggest surprise of all was getting the professor's feedback. Dr. Dean affirmed that not only did I not "get stuck," but she felt like I had embodied the psalmist's words and brought them to life with deep spirit. I will never forget her saying that performing Scripture in this manner has the power to connect with people. She said she would remember this experience and hoped I would too.

She was right. I am continually surprised that every time I open the Bible to Psalm 42, I do not have to read the words; twenty-five years later, I still know every word by heart. When I asked a church member who knows psalms by heart why it was important to her, she said, "You have it with you at all times because you never know when you are going to need it." I have found her words to be true. Over the years, not only have I recited the words of psalms in my own private prayers, but I have also shared them while sitting in a hospital room or standing over a grave with people who are longing for a word. Even if I did not have my Bible with me or was not able to open it as I held their hands, still I could share a comforting word of Scripture— "Where is your God? . . . Hope in God; for I shall again praise him, my help and my God" (Ps 42:3, 5–6)—from my heart to theirs, hoping to unite their thirsty souls to the source of the flowing streams.

The Heart of the Matter

In today's shifting cultural context, people still long for, in Thomas Merton's words, things that are "healthy, certain, and holy," but these things need to be "emphasized and articulated" in imaginative and inspired ways in order for there to be "communication between the hearts and minds of men."[1] This understanding did not come to me from a book or a class. It became clear to me from standing in the pulpit week after week and, in those powerful and equally painful moments, realizing that I wanted and needed to communicate differently in order to connect with the hearts and minds of my listeners.

I remember when I preached one particular sermon that was critically exegeted, creatively conceived, carefully written—and boring. As I stood in the pulpit reading the pages of my manuscript, each page I turned felt heavier. No matter how hard I tried, the sermon never got off the ground. It seemed to sag. And the congregation sagged with it. In her book *The Write Stuff: Crafting Sermons that Capture and Convince*, Sondra Willobee rightly charges, "Collectively, we preachers hold a great number of persons hostage in boredom or frustration when our sermons sag."[2] Fred Craddock goes even further, claiming, "Boredom is a form of evil. It works against the faith by provoking contrary thoughts or lulling to sleep or draping the whole occasion with a pall of indifference."[3] Sagging sermons not only bore individual listeners but collectively communicate that worship is a waste of time, that the church is irrelevant, and tragically, that Christianity can (maybe even should) be ignored. But when the power of preaching is embodied, there is nothing boring about it. "Like Spirit, the flesh is a domain of power," asserts Willobee, and even if preachers are uncomfortable with associating our fleshly natures with our spiritual calling, "preaching is a moment of incarnation, during which the preacher becomes 'God's word made flesh.'"[4] Indeed, preaching is a holy calling, and we preachers must ensure that we do not lose the attention of our listeners and thereby sacrifice the opportunity to proclaim the good news of Jesus Christ.

Some may claim that pastors are busy (which is true) and that there is often not enough time (which is also true), but the pastors I know (including myself) take seriously our call to preach and so willingly and painstakingly put in the time and effort to craft a sermon well. Our conviction and sincerity are not in question. Neither is the quality of the written sermon (most times). Yet preachers spend most of their sermon preparation time writing a manuscript.

When people speak of a piece of paper or a manuscript as a "sermon," however, Justo Gonzalez is very much disturbed, insisting, "A sermon is not a text. A sermon is an event. In that event, the text—whether written, outlined, or completely oral—is just one element. And I am not convinced that it is always the most important element!"[5] Barbara Brown Taylor provides a startling statistic: "According to the experts, about 93 percent of what people get from us is not the words we have so carefully chosen but our own embodiment of the word—the way our voices and bodies do or do not match up with our messages of love and grace and forgiveness."[6] In other words, preachers put most of their effort into the wrong thing—getting the words on paper. Consequently, our preaching usually sags in the performance or lack thereof. But preachers do not want to deliver sagging sermons; we want to proclaim messages that have life in them.

But how do we preach sermons that do not sag, that maintain their integrity under the scrutiny of our cultural shift? How do we use the power of the pulpit to speak to restless people who long for a relevant word today? Cognizant of the time in which we live, in this chapter I reimagine the practice of performing the sermon and describe a process by which the words of the preacher do not just go in one aching ear and out the other but whereby the sermon is imprinted on the longing hearts of our listeners and is meaningful and memorable for our congregations. I am arguing for the importance of preaching sermons by heart, not reciting from a manuscript, using a technique I call "preaching from the heart."

This practice is not something that is done for fifteen minutes in a Sunday morning worship service, but rather, it is a weeklong process that includes time and intention to prepare, practice, and perform. Throughout the week, the preacher prepares by attending to prayer and self-care and by asking and seeking God's presence. On Sunday morning before worship, the preacher practices through articulation (the use of voice) and annotation (the use of pen). In the preaching performance, the preacher who proclaims the sermon through animation of the mind, body, and spirit and who abides in the present moment brings the sermon to life.

Prepare

I remember when I was training to run a marathon. I did not think I could do it. After all, although I enjoyed running, I had never gone farther than 6.2 miles (10K). As I began training, I started off slowly, increasing the distance daily from six to ten to sixteen to twenty miles. Because of the intentional preparation process, I was able to go the distance (26.2 miles) on the day of the marathon. Just like the tortoise in the classic tale, I ran slowly but steadily toward the end, finishing in four hours. As I crossed the finish line of the Marine Corp Marathon in Washington, DC, a Marine officer put a medal around my neck. When I tried to give it back, convinced that I had not won in any of the age categories, he saluted me, saying, "Everyone who finishes the race gets a medal, ma'am. Well done!" Preaching a sermon is not a fifteen-minute sprint on a Sunday morning; it is more like a marathon, a weeklong process that requires not only dedicated exegetical work but also spiritual preparation.

Attend: "Speak Lord, for I am listening"

I remember in my early years of sermon preparation when I was caring for two young children, I would sneak away to my office, sit down at my computer on Saturday and say, "OK, God, I have only two hours before they wake up from their nap; start speaking a word. I am ready to hear it and write it." Over the years, I have learned the value of attending to the sermon as it unfolds in me throughout the week. Preaching from the heart is not a matter of impromptu exhortation or pulling words out of one's robe pocket on Sunday morning.

Preachers must attend to the hard work of prayerfully and intentionally preparing throughout the week. How long will this preparation take? It is different for everyone, but every preacher should take the time necessary to create a meaningful sermon, beginning with reading the text on Monday and journeying with it throughout the week—reflecting, writing, revising, and rehearsing for the performance of the sermon—being careful not to rush through this process just to get a sermon written. Knowing that you will preach without notes makes you prepare in a different way—listening for a word that can be written for the ear as well as preached from the heart, by heart.

The spiritual process of preparation shapes both the sermon and the preacher because preaching is not just about speaking; first and foremost, it is about listening. It is not about filling up the page with words but about first creating space in your work and within yourself to receive the word that will fill you and your congregation.

This preparation is a labor of love. In *Birthing the Sermon*, Jana Childers imagines preaching as "a mother who conceives and gives birth to faith." Even John Calvin goes so far as to compare preachers with wet nurses: "The dissolute nurse wastes her energies and has no milk to give the child, but she who will work readily, and will take food and sustenance, along with her normal rest, she will be able also to feed her baby. So it is with those who have to preach the word of God."[7] Engaged in the painstaking work to conceive and give birth to a sermon, preachers who nourish their own spirits throughout the week will be able to nurture those who come with longing hearts to feed on a lifegiving word, proclaimed and embodied.

Paul Scott Wilson provocatively asks, "Does God start speaking in the moment of delivery or has God been working, performing throughout the preparation process properly understood as a prayerful and scholarly encounter with the biblical text and our world?" He then answers his question: performance in preaching is "not an incarnational moment of giving birth but an incarnational process of the Word becoming flesh."[8] In other words, the preacher's performance of a sermon is not a static moment in time but a dynamic movement through time. When the preacher listens throughout the week for the word God is speaking, the preacher is more likely to hear that word. And when the preacher has been convicted by the word of God herself, then she can expect to convict a congregation. When a preacher has been comforted by the word of God himself, then he will be able to comfort his listeners. Since preachers will be the channel of the sermon, we need to attend to ourselves—body, mind, and spirit. To attend means to pay attention to and to be present with, and it is best done through regular prayer and self-care.

While the preacher is at work on the sermon script, the word of God is also at work on the preacher, revising and rehearsing, between the lines. Furthermore, Wilson suggests, "The preacher is in a sense the initial audience of God's performance and brings forward to the congregation what has been revealed through the week."[9] So how does a preacher get a ticket to God's performance? The preacher can easily get an early, free pass to God's performance through prayer, practiced every day and in many different ways, including through *lectio divina*, contemplative prayer, breath prayer, silent prayer, and body prayer. Prayer cultivates our ground of being and prepares us to nurture the seeds of inspiration, wherever and whenever they may come.

Prayer doesn't have to be poised or polished; it can be messy and mundane. Any prayer will do. It doesn't have to be a beautiful blue iris; it can be weeds, as Mary Oliver reminds us in her poem "Praying." A prayer can be just a few words patched together that make a "doorway into thanks, and a silence in which / another voice may speak."[10] With a simple prayer, like "Speak, Lord, for I am listening," we may hear a word from God—a word to preach to the people of God.

Exercise: Prepare throughout the week by attending to your whole self—body, mind, and spirit—without neglect of the wounds uncovered therein. Whether you walk or bike, garden or golf, eat chocolate or drink wine, read a book or play piano, go to a museum or a party, color with your children or cook a meal for someone, listen to a friend or talk to a therapist—whatever it is, find something that feeds your soul and do it regularly. More often than not, such quotidian practices done with attention promote healing and wholeness and even usher you into the presence of the holy. And those who have been in the presence of the holy will reflect it for those who come to church hoping to hear a word of grace or to see a glimpse of glory.

Ask: "Where have you seen the Lord?"

As a new preacher, my sermon preparation was a desperate plea for divine dictation, but over the years I have learned the value and blessing of starting sermon preparation earlier in the week, attending to it each day, being open to unexpected glimpses of grace. Sometimes these spiritual surprises come in private prayer and other times in community study. In a recent Bible study, we read the Easter account from John's Gospel, in which Mary Magdalene, having witnessed the resurrection, went from the empty tomb to announce, "I have seen the Lord." I asked people in the Bible study, "Where have *you* seen the Lord? In your life, where have you seen the Lord?" And then I listened—at first, to the silence, and then to their answers. Their answers surprised me, delighted me, inspired me, and helped shape my sermon. I remembered some of their answers and I shared them in the sermon. And I trust that the congregation would remember their words of witness too.

An important step in preparation is asking where others have seen the Lord as well as where they have not seen the Lord but long to. Before proclaiming a sermon, a preacher is called to be present with others, in the green pastures and even in the shadows of death, seeking to find glimpses of grace in both places. A preacher who is not afraid to ask others and oneself "Where is God in this?" will be better prepared to bridge the gap between deep prayerful listening and pastoral public witness.

Preparation is not completed once the Scripture text has been exegeted and the sermon manuscript or notes written. The sermon still needs to be prepared to be preached aloud. Pray that your preparation process has been valuable, for as you were shaping the words, you were being shaped by them. Trust that by attending to God's word and asking for evidence of God's presence, you heard a word that will speak to your listeners.

Exercise: Go into the empty sanctuary and sit in a pew. Set a timer for five minutes. Take a breath, say the prayer, "Speak, Lord, for I am listening," and do just that—listen for a still, small voice. After the timer goes off, set it again for five minutes. Now go stand in the pulpit. Imagine someone in the pew asking you the question, "Where have *you* seen the Lord?" and without prepared written words, begin speaking. Speak your words into the space. Speak your truth into the sanctuary. Speak your testimony into the pews. As you prepare yourself, with God alone as your witness, you will become more comfortable speaking from your heart to the hearts of your listeners.

Practice

When I was in fifth grade, I started playing clarinet in the school band. Well, "playing" may be an exaggeration. Let's say, I began trying to play. The band teacher told me that I had potential but needed a lot more practice. And so I practiced at home. I blew into my clarinet as hard as I could, and what came out of it sounded less like a melodious sound and more like a piercing screech. My sisters complained, but what really got my attention was when my dog, Pepper, ran to the other end of the living room, as far as he could go, laid down, put his paws on his ears, and whimpered. This experience was humorous but also humbling, and it taught me two important lessons: (1) pay attention to your listeners—don't make their ears ache; and (2) practice, practice, practice. Although I played the clarinet in the band for only a few months, throughout my life, I have used my voice to sing in choirs and to preach in churches.

Preaching a sermon is comparable to performing music. Charles Bartow asserts, "Bach's *Magnificat* is not sitting there on the page when the conductor opens the score. *Magnificat* is what the musicians and singers will disentangle from the notes; and it is in what the rest of us will hear, feel . . . when the music is played and sung."[11] Likewise, the sermon is not the words written in the manuscript. The sermon is what the preacher proclaims and what the congregation hears and feels as the word is performed. But a memorable performance does not just happen. Just as musicians and singers who care about their craft would not attempt to perform the *Magnificat* without practice, so too a preacher does not preach from the heart without practice. The process consists of two parts—articulation and annotation.

Articulate: "Use your voice"

To articulate means to express (an idea or feeling) fluently or coherently; to pronounce (something) clearly and distinctly. On Sunday morning before worship, the preacher practices the sermon through articulation with the use of the voice. The voice is essential in preaching the word of God. In *The Divine Sound: Christian Proclamation and the Theology of Sound*, Stephen Webb asserts, "It is the sound of Scripture that saves us, not its appearance on the printed page."[12] So it is for preaching.

In "Finding Voice in the Theological School," Richard Ward seeks to do just that—help his students find their preaching voice through vocalization. He reports that through various oral exercises, his students learn significant lessons, including "the sounds released from the page by means of the voice and body are tied to questions of meaning; inflection, pace, and pitch can change a listener's experience of what a text means . . . that the voice (as part of the body) is not simply an instrument for delivering a message; the voice is a probe for exploring its meaning." The practice of articulating a sermon sharpens the interpretation of the biblical text and clarifies the essence of the message. Ward also reports that in the practice of articulation, the student of preaching will discover that "it is possible to be set free from both pulpit and page and therefore use the voice and body more expressively in oral interpretation," because ultimately, "how the sermon is spoken is crucial to a listener's experience of what it will mean."[13] The sermon is limited to not what is said but *how* it is said. And as the preacher attends to how to say something, the meaning of what is said deepens and becomes clearer, to the preacher and to the congregation. The key to bringing together the *what* and the *how* of the sermon is articulation—using your voice to practice the sermon.

The voice can be a powerful instrument for communicating the word of God to the people of God. But it can also get in the way. To ensure that we are not "a noisy gong or a clanging cymbal," but instead that we "speak in the tongues of mortals and angels," requires, according to the apostle Paul, "love" (1 Cor 13:1). And I would say that one way to show love for your listeners is to practice your preaching voice. Even if a sermon has been written for the ear, it still needs to be tested to determine if it will speak to the ear. Because articulation is such an important part of proclamation, it requires the preacher to rehearse the sermon out loud. The more you practice speaking the words, the better you will understand what you are trying to say. And the more you understand your words, the better your listeners will understand. The more fluently you speak, the more coherent the message; the more distinctly you pronounce words, the clearer the meaning becomes.

As you give voice to the sermon, you also listen on behalf of your congregation. Take into account different "ears," including different generations, learning styles, races, ethnicities, cultures, classes, genders, sexual orientations, political affiliations, life experiences, emotions, and levels of faith. As you speak the words, your ears test how the words will be heard. Ask yourself: How do they sound? Do they speak a word from God? Are they words my people can hear? Do the words ring true? How will they sound to aching ears and longing hearts? Will listeners have ears to hear, or will they stop listening?

In order to improve the likelihood that listeners will hear what you hope they will hear requires rehearsal of the sermon and attention to the voice. Although many voice rehearsal techniques exist, I created an acronym in order to make it easier to remember how to attend to your VOICE: Variety, Openness, and Intonation make for a Clear Emphasis.

V: Variety
As you speak your sermon, speak louder and softer to help convey your meaning. Vary the pace of your speech—speeding up and slowing down, pausing to accentuate ideas and allow listeners to reflect and respond, silently or aloud, depending on the cultural context.

O: Openness
Stand up straight to allow open airways and breathe from your diaphragm. Your breathing will sustain your preaching, so learn how to return to it and get support from it.

I: Intonation
Warm up your voice, intoning the alphabet or chanting alleluias or singing a favorite hymn, to release your free-flowing natural voice.

C: Clarity
Clearly pronounce letters, syllables, and words. Vocalize tricky words and articulate multisyllabic words clearly. And remember that the single most important technique for improving clarity is to *slow down*!

E: Emphasis
Emphasize certain phrases and direct voice expression to enhance your interpretation.

Giving sound to the sermon takes practice throughout the process of "writing for the ear," but that culminates on Sunday morning in the space where you will preach. I arrive at the church at least three hours before the worship service, giving myself time to practice my sermon and prepare my voice before anyone else arrives. I go into the empty sanctuary and go through the ritual of turning on the lights, opening the windows (when temperatures are warm) or turning up the heat (when temperatures are cold), filling up the pitcher on the font with water, and moving the flowers. As I prepare the space, I sing and do vocalization exercises to warm up my voice.

When I am ready, I stand in the place where I am going to preach. I stand up straight, take a deep breath, and open myself in prayer, saying, "Good morning, God. I am here. Thank you for being here. Help me speak a word to your people today." Imagining the pews are filled with my listeners, I begin. I read the entire sermon, even if it is not complete, in order to hear it out loud. It is important to get it off the page and into the space, into your voice.

I dedicate an hour or more to practicing my sermon aloud. I vary my voice. I slow down and enunciate words. I speak up and emphasize points. In order to preach from the heart, I need my voice to cooperate. As I speak the words into being, if the sermon speaks to me, if I am challenged or convicted or if it touches my heart, then I trust that, with the help of the Holy Spirt, it will be a word from God's heart to the hearts of my people. Preparing for the performance of articulating the word of God takes significant time and effort. But as Willobee inspires us, "When the words sing together like music, it is worth every drop of sweat."[14]

Exercise: Make a video recording of yourself preaching a sermon, and then watch and listen to it. What do you see? What do you hear? How do you use your VOICE? Do you hear *variety* in volume and pace? Do you see *openness* in posture and breathing? Is there *intonation*—does your voice sound natural and pleasant? Do you *clearly* pronounce words? Is there *emphasis* in certain places that enhances interpretation? What works well? What does not sound the way you want it to? You can learn a lot by hearing the sound of your own voice and making adjustments so that your voice can become a more effective instrument for preaching the word of God.

Annotate: "Use your pen"

Effectively preaching sermons from the heart involves not only articulation with your voice but also annotation with your pen. To annotate is to add notes to a text in order to explain. In this case, to annotate is to mark your sermon text in order to make the layout clearer, the sentences simpler, and the language more compelling. Ultimately, this process will improve the ability of a preacher to proclaim a memorable word to listeners.

Annotating is done not just when writing the sermon but when practicing it aloud. In fact, I do my best editing as I practice saying the sermon out loud. With my red pen, I begin to cross off sentences, substitute words, and if necessary, even change the order of sentences and paragraphs. This is when I test the integrity of the sermon's layout and the effectiveness of the language. If it is not well organized or expressed, that becomes abundantly clear when I am practicing it in order to preach by heart. If I cannot remember the flow or the words, then chances are good neither will my listeners. But it's not too late. Now is the time to annotate.

The first step is to solidify the sermon's layout. Preaching from the heart is not reading from a manuscript, but an anno-tated text can be used as a prompt, especially in the practice session. As you try to anticipate what comes next, you will need some cues. Paul Scott Wilson explains, "Experienced preachers build into a manuscript or outline certain memory devices, key words, sensory details, images, linked thoughts, rhetorical structures, and stories." He continues, "Because these proceed in a certain sequence and designate certain chunks of material, their effect is to lead the preacher's thought and feelings during the performance. The preacher discovers what comes next in part by following a marked path."[15] Some words that can serve as markers on the path include *introduction, question, Bible, theology, refrain, story,* and *good news.* Some phrases written in the margins can help clarify the structure: *tension in the world, tension in the text, good news in the text, good news in the world.* The words will help you test the integrity of your organization and serve as memory prompts. Picturing the layout in your mind is essential in preaching from the heart. Give yourself a road map that you and your listeners can easily follow. Know where you want to go so you have a better chance of getting there. Practice until you know by heart the narrative arc and key sentences that serve as road markers. This process will help encode the markers in your memory, making it easier to preach. Once you have a clear layout, then you can trust your memory, your annotations, and the Holy Spirit to guide you.

The second step is to simplify the sentences. As you speak the sermon aloud, you will hear what sentences need to be changed so that the ears of your listeners can better hear them. Willobee recommends, "Wherever you can, substitute concrete for abstract, specific for general, common for academic. For example, instead of saying, 'A period of unfavorable weather set in,' say, 'It rained every day for a week.' Instead of 'He showed satisfaction as he took possession of his well-earned reward,' write, 'He grinned as he pocketed the coin.'"[16] If the sentence is too long or complicated for you to remember, then chances are good it will not be memorable for your listeners. Look for places to replace long sentences written for the eye with short phrases written for the ear. In one sermon, I simplified several of my long sentences to these short phrases: "Together we are more faithful. More missional. More giving. More prayerful. More loving."

The third step is to clarify the language. Poets, like preachers, claims Kathleen Norris, use incarnational language—"ordinary words that resonate with the senses as they aim for the stars."[17] What we need to say can usually be expressed with ordinary speech consisting of simple words, concrete images, and specific details. Speechwriter Peggy Noonan explains, "Most of the important things you will ever say or hear in your life are composed of simple, good, sturdy words. 'I love you.' 'It's over.' 'It's a boy.' 'We're going to win.' 'He's dead.' . . . Simple words . . . are like pickets in a fence, slim and unimpressive on their own but sturdy and effective when strung together."[18] Ironically, perhaps, preachers are most impactful when they use simple language to express depth, concrete language to communicate transcendence, down-to-earth words to give people a glimpse of heaven. Although preachers speak of things in the heavenly realm, they are most clearly expressed and most likely understood using concrete language.

As you practice your sermon and speak the words, make them as simple as you can. Imagine you are having a conversation with someone, even a child, trying to explain your point in ways that will connect and intrigue and capture attention. While annotating a sermon on Jesus calling his disciples to pick up their cross and follow him, I clarified the language using a simple poetic stanza:

The cross: it's more than a decoration on which to
    stare;
it's more than an object of devotion to wear;
it's more than a symbol of death to despair.
It's the life of discipleship to bear and Christ's love to
    share.

When you solidify the layout, simplify the sentences, and clarify the language, then it becomes possible to learn your sermon and preach it by heart. Sometimes you want to be sure you express something in a particular way—using your own words or those quoted from someone else. You might mark an excerpt from an article and read from it, making it clear you are using someone else's words. Or you might write some key words or phrases on a notecard and tuck it in your Bible if you want to get the words just right.

One way to help you remember the sermon—and ensure it is memorable for your listeners—is to use a recurring refrain. A refrain can keep the sermon moving and give the listeners touchstones to keep them following along. Teresa Fry Brown teaches her students the musicality of preaching: "Repetition is the restatement of sound, word, or phrase for emphasis. It is a means to instill something into people's memory."[19] Black preachers effectively and powerfully utilize this classic preaching form. In fact, Kenyatta Gilbert claims, "without congregational response, there can be no genuine black sermon."[20] Renowned preacher Martin Luther King Jr. exhibited the memorable power of oral proclamation, heard in the cadence of the refrains "I have a dream" and "Let freedom ring." As the listeners hear the sermonic refrain, they can visualize the dream, imagine the sound of freedom ringing, and commit it to memory. In a sermon about

Psalm 23, I turned the focus of my sermon into a memorable recurring refrain: "Sometimes we need a shepherd."

If you have done the work of writing for the ear, then this process of annotating is confirming. My guiding principle is this: Simplify. My rule of thumb is, if I cannot remember a sentence or a move, then it is too long or cumbersome for listeners to find memorable.

Exercise: Pick up your red pen and start annotating your sermon manuscript.

* Solidify layout: In the margin, write one word for each move.
* Simplify sentences: Try turning sentences into phrases.
* Clarify language: Replace abstract with concrete; use alliteration.
* Craft your focus into a memorable refrain.
* Circle key words or underline key phrases that will cue the next move in your sermon.

Now with the annotations, try preaching your sermon again. You will find that you do not need to use the manuscript but can simply follow the annotations. You will be able to preach from the heart.

Perform

Barbara Brown Taylor uses a manuscript when she preaches. Although she writes out a full manuscript, she acknowledges, "By the time I deliver a sermon, it is almost entirely inside of me. The manuscript is there like a musical score, to make sure I don't forget the movement or the tempo, but my goal is not to look at it while I am talking." She admits, "I did prepare for an entirely oral presentation once. . . . When the time for the sermon came, I just stood up, connected with my listeners, and gave a very short homily. It was exhilarating like rappelling for the first time—and I knew that I could learn to do that more often if I took the time. So far, I have not taken the time."[21] Learning to preach without a manuscript does take time and practice, but I can testify, it is exhilarating—not only for the preacher but for the congregation too—as the preacher's animated presence brings the sermon to life.

Animate: "Use your mind, body, and spirit"

On Sunday morning, the preacher seeking to perform an oral embodied sermon goes into the sanctuary early to rehearse. After articulating the words aloud, annotating the moves of the sermon, simplifying the sentences, and clarifying the language, it is time to do the hard work of animating the message. To animate is to bring to life with renewed vigor and the appearance of movement. When the preacher animates the sermon, it comes to life for the listeners. And just like for any performance, it takes practice.

Homiletics professors taught us to be concerned with the sermon's content and, to a lesser extent, its delivery. Delivery includes the preacher's use of mind and body, voice and expression, words and gestures to communicate the sermon. The concept of delivery, while still a part of homiletical discussions, has been encompassed and broadened by an understanding of performance. Delivery and performance occupy overlapping arenas, but the turn toward performance has opened up conversations on the theology of proclamation and embodiment. Amy McCullough, in *Her Preaching Body*, argues for the central role embodiment plays in preaching. In theology (the word becoming flesh) and in practice (the flesh becoming word), proclamation as performance is not just through a voice reading the text of a manuscript. Rather, McCullough concludes, "A sermon truly becomes a sermon when a preacher's embodiment brings it to life."[22]

In *Listening to Listeners*, homileticians draw a generative distinction: "The term 'delivery' could imply no more relationship between congregation and preacher than the parcel service delivery person has with the householders who receive the parcel." In contrast, "embodiment is intended to suggest that the sermon comes alive through the complete self of the preacher." The preacher cannot just mindlessly drop the words at the doorstep of the church, or even on the steps of the chancel, hoping that they are received; instead, in mind, body, and spirit, the preacher animates God's word for the listeners. Animation refers to the process by which the sermon comes to life in the pulpit—or not. The *Listening to Listeners* homiletical case studies report feedback from people in the pew that revealed, "To our eye some modes of embodiment appear to be energizing to the congregation while others have anesthetizing properties."[23] Clearly, we preachers want to energize, not anesthetize our listeners.

So then, how do we embody the message and animate the sermon to uplift our congregation? How do we perform sermons that are meaningful and memorable? As any performer, the preacher employs certain practices, which over time become holy habits. The practice of performing the sermon, embodying words written for the ear and preaching from the heart, involves the preacher's whole being—mind, body, and spirit.

First, performing the sermon engages the mind of the preacher in remembering and delivering the words of the sermon. Although this is not rote memorization, I do memorize certain sentences, to make sure I get the words just right, as a marker for me and for my listeners. Preaching by heart does not mean you need to remember every word. At a basic level, sermons, like conversations, are made up of words and pauses. You have your words ready, but to perform them requires they be delivered in a certain way. When we shift from one point to another within a sermon, we pause. Studies indicate that after a pause, audiences are alert; their attention level is high, and they listen well. Therefore, effective preachers are not afraid to pause. That is how good stories are told. That is how good sermons are preached. Pauses allow listeners to follow you, reflect on your words, and lean into what comes next. And pauses can also help you remember your place.

When my daughter was young, trying to be helpful as she watched me struggle with writing a sermon, she said to me, "Mom, if you forget what you are going to preach, you can always just stop and say, 'Let us pray.'" That is what I do to this day. If I get lost in my sermon, I often just pause, take a breath, say a quick prayer, and then continue, sometimes in a different way than I had planned. I used to think of a pause as a bad thing until a church member told me, "I appreciate how you pause at different places throughout your sermons. It allows me to reflect on what you just said and even hear God speaking a word to me." So while you are preaching from the heart, if you forget what you wanted to say, take a deep breath, pray, and use your mind to remember your next words. But if not, do not worry, just say what does come to you and trust that either you will get back on track or the Spirit will lead you somewhere else you need to go. Trust that what you remember will be remembered as a word from God to the people of God.

Performing the sermon is not just about remembering the words but about delivering them in a memorable way. To improve our writing, we are instructed not to tell but to show with evocative images. The same skill is valuable in preaching. Do not just tell a story, but show people how it looks, sounds, and feels. Barbara Brown Taylor demonstrates the cumulative power of sensory language in a series of examples illustrating the difference between having the right answer and doing the right thing: "A right answer has never picked up a frightened child, or put an ice chip in the mouth of a dying friend. A right answer has never written a check to the Red Cross, or pried up stinking linoleum from a kitchen floor in the ninth ward of New Orleans."[24] Help your listeners to picture the scene; give details so they come alive for people. It is easier to tell a memorable story when you are speaking out loud than when you are thinking reflectively and typing silently on a keyboard. Practice telling the story a few times, but not too many times, to make sure it is not so scripted that it can be a performed interpretation of the narrative. As the Native American proverb attests, "Tell me the facts and I'll learn. Tell me the truth and I'll believe. But tell me a story and it will live in [my] heart forever."[25]

Preaching from the heart engages the mind and also involves the body. Beyond speaking mindful words, we preachers communicate God's word with our bodies; in fact, most of what we communicate comes through our body language. And often, what our bodies communicate differs from the words we speak. Pay attention to your body as you preach. Allow your hands to move naturally, but mindfully, noticing which gestures you make. If you are preaching on the prophet Nathan scolding David, saying, "You are the man" who betrayed God by exploiting his power to abuse and murder but you speak with a smile and open arms, the spoken and embodied messages conflict, and the overall meaning to listeners is confusing. However, when preaching on the women running from the tomb declaring,

"Jesus is risen from the dead," if you raise your arms and smile joyfully, then the harmonization of our bodies and words will communicate a powerful and memorable message. If we understand the fullness of communication, we can better utilize all aspects of the ways we express meaning. Knowing the power of body language, I do not stand behind the pulpit, because I want my whole body—not just from the shoulders up—to be actively engaged in the sermon and visible to the congregation. With animated language, stories, pauses, facial expressions, and hand gestures, preachers can help their sermons take on a life of their own beyond the written manuscript.

Preaching by heart is not only a mindful enterprise, a bodily endeavor, but also a spiritual experience. Performing the sermon by heart is based on the knowledge that the preacher is a channel of God's word but also that the preacher's body is a temple of the Holy Spirit (1 Cor 6:19). In the creation of the world, God blew spirit (*ruach*) into clay (*adamah*) and brought human beings (*adam*) to life. In Hebrew, *ruach* is translated as both breath and spirit. Breath is essential, sustaining us physically and spiritually, animating our bodies and uniting us with God. And yet when we are performing, nerves often get the better of us, and we forget to breathe. Without breath, our voice is not supported, and our words are not strong. We do not want our words to be merely "blowing in the wind"; rather, we want them to carry the word of God to the people of God with volume and vitality and verve.

The sermon is not what is printed on the page; it is the performance during which the faithful preacher approaches the pulpit with humility and releases one's words, trusting that God's word will be heard through what is said and done, sometimes even in spite of what is said and done. "Part of giving oneself over to God in the preaching act," Paul Scott Wilson admits, "is letting go of the sermon as an act of one's love and labor." But preaching is not one-sided. As Wilson so aptly describes, "The preacher gives the sermon as an offering, lets it go, and leaves not empty-handed, but with the experience of having received the Word even through the giving of it."[26] In the preaching moment, whether we pray, "May the words of my mouth and the meditations of our hearts be acceptable in your sight," or we sing, "Spirit of the Living God, fall afresh on me," or we confess, "Take, O, take me as I am," we give ourselves over to the preaching performance experience prayerfully and faithfully. In this act of giving, we receive and, we trust, so too will our congregations.

Exercise: Practice a sermon you preached recently. Try standing outside the pulpit. Imagine people in the pews. Remember your message and try to preach the sermon without looking at your manuscript. Don't be afraid to use different words. Don't be afraid to pause. Use gestures. Breathe. Through your mind, body, and spirit, let the Holy Spirit animate your words to be the word of God.

Abide: "Use your presence"

Performing the sermon by heart is based on the awareness that the word of God is embodied in and revealed through the mind, body, and spirit of the preacher. The theology of the incarnation reveals a God who is not limited by words but communicates powerfully in the word made flesh. Through Jesus—named Emmanuel, "God with us"—God chooses to be present with us. When preachers step forward to proclaim that truth, they enter into what Alyce McKenzie calls "a dynamic context in which to preach sermons that move from talking about God to evoking God's new possibilities, from the delivery of concepts to the embodiment of divine presence." In the sacred space in which preachers stand—the thin place between heaven and earth—we do not just recite God's word; we reflect God's glory. "We have seen how recent homiletical reflection has emphasized that the goal of preaching is not so much to explain God as to invite listeners into the divine presence and to evoke wonder and possibility," claims McKenzie, but then she honestly admits, "Easier said than done."[27]

Preachers invite listeners into the divine presence when we are in that presence ourselves. Present in the moment. In the space. In your body. To the active Spirit. To the living and speaking God. To your congregation. You and your listeners and the Holy Spirit are all active participants in this sermon-dialogue. You do not have to do all the work yourself. Trust that the people and the Spirit are with you and that they will help you. As you preach, be aware of the faces of the people in the pews. As you see them, think to yourself, "I wonder how I could say this differently . . . to Ed, whose wife just died . . . to Angela, whose son is in rehab . . . to Chris, who has more doubt than faith." Dialogue with listeners during the sermon. But in order to do that, you have to be fully present, open to receive a word from God's heart and share it with the hearts of your listeners. That is the power and presence of preaching from the heart. Preaching from the heart, without reading a manuscript, allows you to be fully present—in mind, body, and spirit. And if you are fully present, then chances are your listeners will be too. And they will remember what you said or, even more, they will remember their experience of being in God's presence.

In the end, we all know that a sermon is more than words. "A sermon is something that happens between people who have consented to spend (at least) a morning of their lives together, listening to one another's stomachs growl, and breathing the same air. A sermon is something that happens in the context of worshiping God," maintains Barbara Brown Taylor. "You really do have to be there."[28] Preaching from the heart allows you to really be there.

Sondra Willobee expresses the preacher's deepest hope and most ardent prayer before the sermon performance: "When a sermon works, when we can see in our hearers' eyes and faces that they are listening, when our sermon moves them to a deeper faith or decisive commitment, and when, by the power at work within us, the sermon accomplishes abundantly far more than we could ask or imagine, it is pure joy!"[29] That is the Spirit at work. And we say, "Thanks be to God."

Exercise: Read and reflect on Jesus's words of commissioning and blessing: "Go therefore and make disciples . . . teaching them . . . and remember I am with you always" (Matthew 28:19-20). Trust that Jesus's promise to be with you and abide with you is true, perhaps especially true when you preach God's word. Now, go and make disciples and teach them. Abide in the present moment, let go of your manuscript and try preaching your sermon by heart. Trust the Spirit to speak a word through you that declares and demonstrates, "God is with us." Always.

Conclusion

For such a time as this, it is necessary for there to be communication between human hearts and God's heart, between the words of the preacher and the ear of the listener. To that end, I recover an oral embodied homiletic and describe a proven method by which the words of the preacher would be emphasized in such a way that they will not go in the listener's one aching ear and out the other, but whereby the sermon would be imprinted on the longing hearts of listeners today.

Since I have changed my method to "writing for the ear" and "preaching from the heart," I can testify that the conversations I have with people at the door have changed from superficial ("Good sermon, preacher") to substantive ("Thank you for your words of encouragement and the perspective on the Good Samaritan—that we could be the person in the ditch and it is Jesus who helps us"; "How comforting"; "Thank you for your gift of kindness and leadership"). I consistently learn that my message was heard, the listener connected with it, and in this case, the listener also received the gift of kindness and leadership. When someone appreciates me for saying something they needed to hear, instead of simply thanking them, I often ask, "What did you hear? What spoke to you?" I am often humbled and sometimes surprised by what they tell me blessed them. Knowing that I did not exactly say what they heard, I simply thank God for speaking through me a word they most needed to hear, from God's heart to their heart. A word they will remember.

I remember when I went back to visit Oak Grove Presbyterian Church in Retreat, New Jersey, the church I had served as pastor fifteen years before. It was good to catch up with people I had not seen in a long time and to share memories and updates on our families. When most people had left, Chuck pulled me aside. He asked, "Do you remember the day when you gave us water beads to carry with us?" I did remember giving out water beads from the baptismal font in that church and other churches I have served since. I will never forget what Chuck did next. He pulled a water bead out of his pocket and said, "Here is the water bead you gave to me. I have carried this bead every day in my pocket for the last fifteen years. I will always remember the sermon you preached that day about how important it is to remember our baptisms and how much God loves us." In this story of the water bead in Chuck's pocket and the word of grace in his heart, we witness the power of preaching to communicate a memorable word that changes hearts and minds for good.

In this complex world and changing church, it is my hope that this book will equip and inspire preachers to preach sermons that are engaging and memorable—that they will go beyond words written on a page to words inscribed on the hearts of listeners longing for a life-giving word to remember. While it may seem presumptuous to think that we share in the divine enterprise of speaking a word that created the world, carved the covenant, and culminated in Christ, I am confident that as preachers we do. When we proclaim the word of God, we tell the story of God's relentless love for God's people. And when we preach in meaningful and memorable ways that communicate to aching ears today, we participate in changing the world for good, and for God, one longing heart at a time. May it be so.

NOTES

Introduction

1. Malala Yousafzai with Christina Lamb, *I Am Malala: The Story of the Girl Who Stood up for Education and Was Shot by the Taliban* (New York: Little, Brown, 2016), 192.

Chapter 1

1. Thomas Merton to Paulo Alceu Amoroso Lima, Rio de Janeiro, November 1961, in *Cold War Letters*, ed. Christine M. Bochen and William H. Shannon (Maryknoll, NY: Orbis, 2006), 12.
2. David J. Lose, *Preaching at the Crossroads: How the World and Our Preaching Is Changing* (Minneapolis: Fortress, 2013), 5, 6.
3. Walter Brueggemann, *Practice of Prophetic Imagination: Preaching an Emancipating Word* (Minneapolis: Fortress, 2012), 2–4.
4. "In U.S., Decline of Christianity Continues at Rapid Pace: An Update on America's Changing Religious Landscape," Pew Research Center, October 17, 2019, https://tinyurl.com/y54m8cjv.
5. Irving Kristol, commentary on *The Protestant Era*, by Paul Tillich, *Commentary Magazine*, March 1949, https://tinyurl.com/y3jxjfwc.
6. Lose, *Preaching at the Crossroads*, 32.
7. Diana Butler Bass, *Christianity after Religion: The End of Church and the Birth of a New Spiritual Awakening* (New York: HarperOne, 2013), 53, 59, 92.

8. Nicholas Carr, *The Shallows: What the Internet Is Doing to Our Brains* (New York: W. W. Norton, 2011), 152.

9. Nicholas Kristof, "We're Less and Less a Christian Nation, and I Blame Some Blowhards," *New York Times*, October 26, 2019, https://tinyurl.com/y3essqna.

10. Bass, *Christianity after Religion*, 51.

11. Krista Tippett in a discussion with journalists who write and speak about religion, led by Stephen Prothero, chair of the Department of Religion at Boston University. "Religious Literacy: What Every American Should Know," Pew Research Center, December 3, 2007, https://tinyurl.com/yxj6cehw.

12. Fred Craddock, "Inductive Preaching Renewed," in *The Renewed Homiletic*, ed. O. Wesley Allen Jr. (Minneapolis: Fortress, 2010), 48.

13. Lose, *Preaching at the Crossroads*, 111.

14. Neil Postman, *Amusing Ourselves to Death: Public Discourse in the Age of Show Business* (New York: Penguin, 2005), 33.

15. Postman, 63.

16. Robert MacNeil, "Is Television Shortening Our Attention Span?," *New York University Education Quarterly* 14, no. 2 (Winter 1983): 2, cited in Postman, *Amusing Ourselves to Death*, 105.

17. Postman, *Amusing Ourselves to Death*, 42.

18. Allen, "The Pillars of the New Homiletic," in Allen, *Renewed Homiletic*, 4.

19. Allen, 18.

20. Clyde E. Fant, *Preaching for Today* (San Francisco: Harper & Row, 1987), 159.

21. Marshall McLuhan, *Understanding Media: The Extensions of Man* (Boston: MIT Press, 1994), 7. See also McLuhan, *The Gutenberg Galaxy* (Toronto, ON: University of Toronto Press, 1962); and McLuhan, *The Medium Is the Message: An Inventory of Effects* (Ann Arbor, MI: University of Michigan Press, 1996).

22. Walter J. Ong, *The Presence of the Word* (New Haven, CT: Yale University Press, 1967), 21, 23.

23. Postman, *Amusing Ourselves to Death*, 117.

24. Fant, *Preaching for Today*, 165, 163.

25. Alyce M. McKenzie, *Making a Scene in the Pulpit: Vivid Preaching for Visual Learners* (Louisville, KY: Westminster John Knox, 2018), 23, cover.
26. Postman, *Amusing Ourselves to Death*, 121, 122.
27. Fant, *Preaching for Today*, 171, 172.
28. Fred Craddock, *Preaching* (Nashville: Abingdon, 1985), 191–92.
29. Eugene Lowry, *Doing Time in the Pulpit* (Nashville: Abingdon, 1985), 102.
30. Lowry, "Narrative Renewed," in Allen, *Renewed Homiletic*, 96.
31. Brian McLaren, *Everything Must Change* (Nashville: Thomas Nelson, 2007), 2–3.

Chapter 2

1. Linda A. Mercadante, *Belief without Borders: Inside the Minds of the Spiritual but Not Religious* (New York: Oxford, 2014).
2. Merton, *Cold War Letters*, 12.
3. Francis Brown, S. R. Drive, and Charles Briggs, *A Hebrew and English Lexicon of the Old Testament* (Oxford: Clarendon, 1906), 269–70.
4. Walter Bauer, *A Greek-English Lexicon of the New Testament and Other Early Christian Literature*, trans. and ed. William F. Arndt and F. Wilbur Gingrich, 2nd ed. (Chicago: University of Chicago Press, 1979), 522.
5. Emily A. Holmes, *Flesh Made Word: Medieval Women Mystics, Writing, and the Incarnation* (Waco, TX: Baylor University Press, 2013), 1.
6. Jon L. Berquist, *Incarnation* (St. Louis: Chalice, 1999), 3, 83.
7. Berquist, 88, 89.
8. Holmes, *Flesh Made Word*, 13, 32.
9. Holmes, 45.
10. John Hick, *The Metaphor of God Incarnate: Christology in a Pluralistic Age*, 2nd ed. (Louisville, KY: Westminster John Knox, 2005), 178.
11. Holmes, *Flesh Made Word*, 45.
12. Holmes, 22, 18, 14.
13. Karoline Lewis, "Commentary on John 1:1–14," Working Preacher, December 25, 2016, https://tinyurl.com/y5rg3fs6.

14. Kathleen Norris, *Amazing Grace: A Vocabulary of Faith* (New York: Riverhead, 1998), 31.
15. Holmes, *Flesh Made Word*, 33.
16. Charles L. Bartow, *God's Human Speech: A Practical Theology of Proclamation* (Grand Rapids, MI: Eerdmans, 1997), 3, 27.
17. Berquist, *Incarnation*, 82.
18. Bartow, *God's Human Speech*, 2.
19. Presbyterian Church (U.S.A.), "The Second Helvetic Confession," in *The Constitution of the Presbyterian Church (U.S.A.)*, part 1, *Book of Confessions* (Louisville, KY: Office of the General Assembly, 2016), sec. 5.004, p. 77.
20. Amy P. McCullough, *Her Preaching Body: Conversations about Identity, Agency, and Embodiment among Contemporary Female Preachers* (Eugene, OR: Cascade, 2018), 12–13, 6.
21. McCullough, 98.
22. William Willimon, "Personification," in *Preaching the Incarnation*, ed. Peter K. Stevenson and Stephen I. Wright (Louisville, KY: Westminster John Knox, 2010), 33–34. Used with the permission of William Willimon.

Chapter 3

1. Merton, *Cold War Letters*, 12.
2. Lowry, "Narrative Renewed," 91.
3. Fant, *Preaching Today*, 163–64.
4. Lowry, "Narrative Renewed," 91.
5. Fant, *Preaching Today*, 165.
6. Fant, 173.
7. Dave McClellan, *Preaching by Ear: Speaking God's Truth from the Inside Out* (Wooster, MA: Weaver, 2014), 132–33. McClellan adopts the method of Marcus Quintilian, ancient Roman educator and rhetorician.
8. Karyn L. Wiseman, "Writing for the Ear," in *Writing Theologically: Foundations for Learning*, ed. Eric D. Barreto (Minneapolis: Fortress, 2015), 34, 43.

9. Barbara Brown Taylor, *The Preaching Life* (Lanham, MD: Rowman & Littlefield, 1993), 49, 15.

10. Thomas H. Troeger and Leonora Tubbs Tisdale, *A Sermon Workbook: Exercises in the Art and Craft of Preaching* (Nashville: Abingdon, 2013), 38.

11. John S. McClure et al., *Listening to Listeners: Homiletical Case Studies* (St. Louis: Chalice, 2004), 5.

12. Fred Craddock, *As One without Authority* (St. Louis: Chalice, 2001), 18.

13. Thomas G. Long, *The Witness of Preaching*, 3rd ed. (Louisville, KY: Westminster John Knox, 2016), 127, 137.

14. David Buttrick, *Homiletic: Moves and Structures* (Minneapolis: Fortress, 1987), 305, 37, 28.

15. Stephen Farris, *So, Tell Me a Story: The Art of Storytelling for Preaching and Teaching* (Eugene, OR: Cascade, 2018), 1, 4.

16. N. T. Wright, *The Original Jesus: The Life and Vision of a Revolutionary* (Grand Rapids, MI: Eerdmans, 1996), 36.

17. Charles L. Rice, "Storytelling Renewed," in Allen, *Renewed Homiletic*, 22.

18. Thomas G. Long, "Out of the Loop: The Changing Practice of Preaching," in *What's the Shape of Narrative Preaching? Essays in Honor of Eugene L. Lowry*, ed. Mike Graves and David J. Schlafer (St. Louis: Chalice, 2008), 126.

19. McKenzie, *Making a Scene*, 78.

20. Anna Carter Florence, *Preaching as Testimony* (Louisville, KY: Westminster John Knox, 2007), xiii, 121, 135.

21. Kenyatta Gilbert, *Exodus Preaching: Crafting Sermons about Justice and Hope* (Nashville: Abingdon, 2018), 90.

22. Teresa L. Fry Brown, *Delivering the Sermon: Voice, Body, and Animation in Proclamation*, ed. O. Wesley Allen Jr. (Minneapolis: Fortress, 2008), 8.

23. Langston Hughes, "The Weary Blues," Poetry Foundation, 2002, https://tinyurl.com/y9clzpc2; Audre Lorde, "Who Said It Was Simple," Poetry Foundation, 1973, https://tinyurl.com/y2tys83t; and Maya Angelou, "Caged Bird," Poetry Foundation, 1983, https://tinyurl.com/ycx5bnee.

NOTES

24. Sondra B. Willobee, *The Write Stuff: Crafting Sermons That Capture and Convince* (Louisville, KY: Westminster John Knox, 2009), 97–98.
25. Barbara Brown Taylor, "Bothering God," in *Birthing the Sermon: Women Preachers on the Creative Process*, ed. Jana Childers (St. Louis: Chalice, 2001), 161.
26. Troeger and Tisdale, *Sermon Workbook*, 116.
27. Troeger and Tisdale, 117.

Chapter 4

1. Merton, *Cold War Letters*, 12.
2. Willobee, *Write Stuff*, 2.
3. Fred B. Craddock, *Overhearing the Gospel* (Nashville: Abingdon, 1978), 13.
4. Willobee, *Write Stuff*, 94.
5. Justo L. Gonzalez, "A Hispanic Perspective: By the Rivers of Babylon," in *Preaching Justice: Ethnic and Cultural Perspectives*, ed. Christine Marie Smith (Cleveland, OH: United Church Press, 1998), 80; Troeger and Tisdale, *Sermon Workbook*, 117.
6. Taylor, "Bothering God," 160.
7. Jana Childers, introduction to *Birthing the Sermon*, ix, quoting John Calvin's Sermon XXI.
8. Paul Scott Wilson, "Preaching, Performance, and the Life and Death of 'Now,'" in *Performance in Preaching: Bringing the Sermon to Life*, ed. Jana Childers and Clayton J. Schmit (Grand Rapids, MI: Baker Academic, 2008), 43.
9. Wilson, 43.
10. Mary Oliver, *Devotions: The Selected Poems of Mary Oliver* (New York: Penguin, 2017), 131.
11. Bartow, *God's Human Speech*, 64.
12. Stephen Webb, *The Divine Voice: Christian Proclamation and the Theology of Sound* (Grand Rapids, MI: Brazos, 2004), 177.
13. Richard Ward, "Finding Voice in Theological School," in Childers and Schmit, *Performance in Preaching*, 147.

14. Willobee, *Write Stuff*, 100.
15. Wilson, "Life and Death," 47.
16. Willobee, *Write Stuff*, 95.
17. Kathleen Norris, "Incarnational Language," *Christian Century*, July 30–August 6, 1997, 699.
18. Peggy Noonan, *Simply Speaking: How to Communicate Your Ideas with Style, Substance, and Clarity* (New York: Harper Collins, 1998), 50–51.
19. Brown, *Delivering the Sermon*, 37.
20. Kenyatta Gilbert, *The Journey and Promise of African American Preaching* (Minneapolis: Fortress, 2011), 23.
21. Taylor, "Bothering God," 161.
22. McCullough, *Her Preaching Body*, 98, 97. For more on homiletic scholars' turn to performance, see Jana Childers, *Performing the Word: Preaching as Theatre* (Nashville: Abingdon, 1998), 42–43; Ronald Allen, *Preaching: An Essential Guide* (Nashville: Abingdon, 2002), 107; and Alyce M. McKenzie, "At the Intersection of *Actio Divina* and *Homo Performans*: Embodiment and Evocation," in Childers and Schmit, *Performance in Preaching*, 55.
23. McClure et al., *Listening to Listeners*, 14.
24. Willobee, *Write Stuff*, 95, quoting Barbara Brown Taylor, "Do This and You Will Live," (sermon, Festival of Homiletics, Atlanta, GA, April 17, 2006).
25. "Traditional Storytelling," Education, RiverWinds, 2019, https://www.theriverwinds.com/education.
26. Wilson, "Life and Death," 47.
27. McKenzie, "At the Intersection of *Actio Divina*," 57, 58.
28. Taylor, "Bothering God," 162.
29. Willobee, *Write Stuff*, 7.

Working Preacher Books is a partnership between Luther Seminary, WorkingPreacher.org, and Fortress Press.

Books in the Series

Preaching from the Old Testament by Walter Brueggemann

Leading with the Sermon by William H. Willimon

The Gospel People Don't Want to Hear: Preaching Challenging Sermons by Lisa Cressman

A Lay Preacher's Guide: How to Craft a Faithful Sermon by Karoline M. Lewis

Preaching Jeremiah: Announcing God's Restorative Passion by Walter Brueggemann

Preaching the Headlines: Pitfalls and Possibilities by Lisa L. Thompson

Honest to God Preaching: Talking Sin, Suffering, and Violence by Brent A. Strawn

Writing for the Ear, Preaching from the Heart by Donna Giver-Johnston

The Peoples' Sermon: Preaching as a Ministry of the Whole Congregation by Shauna K. Hannan

Donna Giver-Johnston's sermons may be viewed at http://cpcba.squarespace.com/sermons.